'Anne-Louise offers an ant
measure the value of life by
she shows us how to live mea
day by day, finding contentr
trusting that "small acts can achieve great results". Honest,
down-to earth and compassionate, she encourages us to face
the often less-than-ideal realities of life with faith and
hopefulness. Every lesson learnt (and there are many)
becomes an opportunity to comfort others with the comfort
she has discovered in Christ's love. This is a timely reminder
that God's kingdom isn't built through grand schemes or
strategies but by the obedient, faithful sowing of seed in the
often ordinary places life takes us.'
Becky Silver, Presenter, BBC Radio 4 Daily Service

'Anne-Louise thoughtfully combines lessons drawn from the
Bible with her own wide pastoral experience to give a wise
and accessible guide to pastoral care. There are insights,
encouragement and challenges for anyone engaged in this
ministry. Her open and clear writing style models the care
she describes. I warmly recommend this book.'
*Revd Philip Rowe, Pastoral Care Lead of Christ Church
Downend, formerly Area Dean of Bristol West in the Diocese of
Bristol*

'This very readable book brings together biblical themes with
the writer's wide pastoral and personal experience. It
provides "sanctified common sense". I have personally learnt
much from *Slowing Down* and will carry many points
through to my own lay ministry and particularly my
bereavement/funeral visits.'
Travers Harpur, lay minister in the Diocese of Chelmsford

'We may find ourselves slowing down in our older years, but this does not prevent us from continuing to be useful in God's service. Indeed, slowing down will help us to listen to others, reflect on God's goodness and faithfulness and focus on what is really important in life. This helpful book by Anne-Louise Critchlow, reflecting a lifetime of practical wisdom honed by God's grace and His Spirit, will encourage you on in your service of Christ. The questions at the end of each chapter are practical and searching and will help you to discern what God is saying to you. I thoroughly recommend this book.'
Peter Misselbrook, retired Baptist minister and former data analyst for the Bible Society

'An inspiring read full of powerful anecdotes, personal spiritual lessons and rich godly advice. In *Slowing Down*, Anne-Louise illustrates through many personal and sometimes painful episodes the faithfulness and redemptive work of our God.'
Paul Barnett, elder at Gateway New Frontiers Church, Dorset; ex-crime scene investigator; Truth Be Told worker in a dementia care home

Slowing Down

Finding beauty in the slow lanes of life

Anne-Louise Critchlow

instant
apostle

First published in Great Britain in 2025

Instant Apostle
104A The Drive
Rickmansworth
Herts
WD3 4DU

Every effort has been made to seek permission to use copyright material reproduced in this book. The publisher apologises for those cases where permission might not have been sought and, if notified, will formally seek permission at the earliest opportunity.

The views and opinions expressed in this work are those of the author and do not necessarily reflect the views and opinions of the publisher.

British Library Cataloguing-in-Publication Data

A catalogue record for this book is available from the British Library.

This book and all other Instant Apostle books are available from Instant Apostle:

Website: www.instantapostle.com

Email: info@instantapostle.com

ISBN 978-1-912726-89-9

Printed in Great Britain.

To my wonderful husband Mark, who has always encouraged me to slow down – not always very successfully!

Some names and details have been changed for anonymity

Contents

Preface

'Slow Down!' flashed the sign in neon light against the night sky. All the cars in the street, including mine, were rushing around, seemingly oblivious to the warning.

Then I woke up.

Immediately I had a strong feeling that this dream was from God and that it contained warning and instruction.

Slow Down? Surely not me? I had plenty of energy. Why me? I still had so many things I wanted to achieve.

As I reflected, my head still on the pillow and drowsy with sleep, I knew why. I needed more time to be with my family, both the youngest generation of grandchildren and the oldies. I needed time to listen to people in my community. I needed to take life at a slower pace for the sake of my own physical and mental wellbeing. I needed time to reflect and think about the meaning of my life. I needed time to listen to God and to pray.

I knew that my dream contained a clear instruction.

Speed awareness

The sense that God was already speaking to me about this had begun a few weeks earlier in a very down-to-earth experience which is familiar to so many of us in our day-to-day lives.

I had received two speeding tickets in a week, one in the Midlands, where I had been working, and one nearer home. The Bristol ticket had seemed the most unfair. Shortly after leaving the M32 motorway, drivers approach the 30mph speed limit in the built-up area of Bristol, but sandwiched in between these areas is one road where the speed limit is reduced to 20mph. I had hardly noticed it. I had to disagree with the wayside rhyme, 'Twenty is plenty.' Not in my experience. I just wanted to get home as quickly as possible.

With one fine paid and points notched up on my licence, I had no alternative but to register for a speed awareness course, which meant giving up three hours of my 'precious' time, as I perceived it to be. I couldn't even cheat (a big temptation) by doing some work or emailing on the side, because I had to keep answering questions or giving an opinion. The organisers were obviously well versed in dealing with would-be skivers like me.

The first most annoying thing about the course was how long it took just to get underway, with each participant giving a personal introduction, and the rationale of the course being explained in detail. With my usual impatience, I just wanted to do the bare necessary to pass the course. In my not so humble opinion, I didn't really need to learn how to drive better because I was already so good at it! My husband and children might have a few negative things to say about my skill behind the wheel but, hey, family members are always prejudiced against a mum driving, aren't they?

I sat there and fumed my way through the course. The facilitator's habits annoyed me. He repeated the person's name after every answer, just like the good salesman he had been trained to be. He had something irritatingly positive to say about every response, however simplistic. It went something like this:

Trainer: How do you know what the speed limits are in an area?

Participant: Because the speed limit is marked on the lampposts.

Trainer: Absolutely right, John. I can see you've been noticing those posts.

I didn't know whether to scream in frustration or to laugh out loud. All I knew was that I wanted to finish this ridiculous course and get on with the important things of life, like doing my job.

However, as the first hour went by, I began to find that I had a few things to learn. My fellow speeders seemed to be tolerant and good humoured and even showed appreciation of the trainer's style.

And then two facts were proved by statistics, graphs and examples. Speeding even on the motorway would not get you to your destination any faster. The difference between doing an emergency stop at 30mph and 20mph is huge, especially when it comes to serious injury of a child stepping out in front of a car. Such terrible accidents also have a huge effect on the mental health of the driver.

The course instructor demonstrated that the only way to get to a destination on time is to prepare properly the night before and to start punctually. Oh dear! This was against my habit of throwing everything in a bag at the last minute and rushing out of the door on my way to Plymouth or Birmingham.

The whole course, which I had despised at the beginning, had a radical effect on my driving and my organisational habits.

Spiritual discipline

The more I thought about it afterwards, the more I realised that my enforced attendance on the speed awareness course was like spiritual discipline.

'No discipline seems pleasant at the time,' says the writer to the Hebrews (12:11). He is right there. It doesn't, and I instinctively don't appreciate it! But Hebrews 12:5-6 makes some good points:

> Do not make light of the Lord's discipline,
> and do not lose heart when he rebukes you,
> because the Lord disciplines the one he loves.

Verses 10 and 11 of the same chapter continue with this theme.

> God disciplines us for our good, that we may share
> in his holiness. No discipline seems pleasant at the
> time, but painful. Later on, however, it produces a
> harvest of righteousness and peace for those who
> have been trained by it. (NIV 1984)

I had no choice but to attend the speed awareness course, and we Christians have no choice in enduring the difficulties and trials of life which God allows to come our way. Just as I fretted against the inconvenience of spending three hours on the course, I often fret against the corrections and lessons God wants to teach me. Nowadays, when I get to that annoying 20mph stretch of road after the motorway, I consciously slow down. Apart from anything else, I don't want to do another speed awareness course or get another fine! But I do remember what I learned about driving. Similarly, what God has taught me through the trials and failures of my life, I have not easily forgotten. We all inherit unhelpful characteristics of personality through our family DNA, and I am no exception. When my life has been in the 'go slow' lane I have understood my weaknesses. Of course, I also inherited positive qualities which God can use, but it's the lessons from the hard knocks of life which have been the most enduring.

The purpose of this book

So, part of this book is sharing what God has been teaching me as He has admonished me with, 'Slow down!' These lessons come from different stages of my life, and I have tried to explain as honestly as I can about some of the tussles I have experienced. My life has not been particularly dramatic – I'm not a converted drug dealer, neither am I an influencer, but I have tried to explain what I have found difficult. My personality is such that I don't accept the reality of life passively. This book will tell you about some of my weaknesses and how God has dealt with them. It will show you that I have been rebellious and difficult and slow to recognise my own faults, keen to point out the speck in someone else's eye when the reality has been that I've failed to notice the great whopping 'plank' in my own (Matthew 7:5). I'm not naturally submissive. It's a story of how I've failed so often to 'count others better than [myself]' (Philippians 2:3, RSV).

It's also about the sufferings I've seen others go through and what a challenge that has been to my Christian life. Sometimes it's hard to be a believer when you see how much others have suffered, and I have included some examples for reflection.

In visiting older people, I've met some who've given up on the faith and become disillusioned, but we can reassure such people that God has not given up on them. I know that, because God, in His mercy, has not given up on me. If the challenges in both my character and my circumstances resonate with you, then I hope that you will be encouraged to believe that God won't give up on you either. I've always believed that God responds to our honesty, both before we become believers and during our Christian lives. God does business with us in a very down-to-earth manner and exposes our true motivation for our actions.

It is also a book about pastoral ministry. Sometimes churches make this a very official job. I think there is a tendency to professionalise so much in our society, and that tendency has crept into the life of the Church in all denominations. It's clearly important to have safeguarding rules in place to protect the vulnerable among those who are visiting and the visited, and official training can be very useful, but encouraging and helpful conversations can take place in the most unlikely and 'unofficial' situations. It can also be the person who is supposed to be 'helped' who can turn out to be 'the helper'. Recently, when I was acting in an official capacity as a 'spiritual advisor', the person I was advising prayed something which was relevant for my own guidance in a difficult situation. It was a role reversal which showed the

Holy Spirit to be at work in a helpful way. On another occasion, I wasn't offering mentorship in any way. After I had preached in church one Sunday, I was drinking coffee alongside someone I didn't know. A chance question combined with the person's own reflections about the sermon drew out from them observations about their grieving process which they told me they had found helpful to express. On neither of these occasions was the person offering advice doing anything officially. But I felt the guidance of the Holy Spirit in both encounters, both when I was being helped and when the other person was responding to a sermon through self-discovery. Whether you are working for a living, or are a volunteer, or are a Christian going about your everyday life, you may well have similar experiences.

The gift of 'helps'

When we share who we are honestly, not pretending to have all the answers, we can practise the gift of 'helps' (1 Corinthians 12:28, KJV). Perhaps it doesn't seem a very glamorous gift – some of the others in the list of gifts in 1 Corinthians 12 seem far more attractive. But there are benefits to sharing with others who we really are. Paul tells us that 'we have this treasure in jars of clay to show that this all-surpassing power is from God and not from us' (2 Corinthians 4:7). I know that jars of clay break quite easily, but when they are scattered in pieces on the ground, we see the 'treasure' that was inside them. The power of the Holy Spirit and the love of the Lord Jesus are far more important and effective than our clay jars.

Before I ever had a named ministry in a church (either as a lay minister or as an ordained one), I found that people would open up to me, sometimes on public transport or in the supermarket, or in the school corridors and during break times when I was a teacher (both staff and pupils), or in Marseille when I was part of a church planting team,[1] or as the coordinator and a street worker of our local Street Pastors team in Salford.[2] It was never a position I sought. It just happened – proof, I think, of an unsought gift from God. It is a gift that can be used in an official ministry, and we can all benefit from training and guidance, but you will gradually discover whether you have it or not. Isaiah 61:1 tells us that 'the LORD has anointed me … to bind up the broken-hearted'. This is part of a prophecy spoken by Jesus about the work He would do on this earth (see Luke 4:18-19; Isaiah 61:1-2), but in a small way, it is part of what we are called to do as Christians. If you find yourself in a similar situation, then this book is for you.

There is a danger that we can be too self-important; alternatively, we could become busy-bodies and clearly not the answer to everybody's need for advice, but if the gift of 'helps' is truly there, we will not see ourselves as overly important, and will know when to withdraw from someone's life, either for their sake or for our own

---

[1] The Gospel Literature Outreach was founded in 1963 by Colin Tilsley and involved in church planting in Europe from 1974. Glo-europe.org (accessed 4th December 2024). Church planting involves starting a church in a place, where, as yet, there is no collective witness. My husband and I were involved in a church-planting team in Marseille between 1979 and 1981.

[2] Street Pastors with parent organisation, Ascension Trust, was founded in 2023 by Les Isaacs. www.streetpastors.org (accessed 4th December 2024).

wellbeing. We can be truly guided by the Holy Spirit in the way we exercise the gift of 'helps'. I know several people in our church and among my friends who exercise this gift without any official label. I value my conversations with them.

If you are an official 'pastoral visitor' in your church and find that God is increasingly using you in that ministry, or if you are discovering that you have the gift of 'helps' or 'helping', or 'wisdom' (1 Corinthians 12:8), then this book is for you. You may well seek to do more official pastoral training, and that will be useful, but I am hopeful that this book might lead you to more personal reflections and be a help, even if you never go on an official course.

Ministering among older people

In the last seven years I have been a chaplain for older people, both for a secular national housing and care home charity and as an Anna Chaplain for my church and in north-east Bristol.[3] There are many active retired people, as well as younger people, involved in this sort of work up and down the country. This book is particularly for you, and many of the examples in this book come from this area of ministry. There is much need in our society for those who can visit older people, especially those who are lonely and isolated.

Our later lives are built on the experiences of our younger lives, and so this book is also useful for those who 'counsel' any age group. The more like Jesus we become,

---

[3] Anna Chaplaincy (part of Bible Reading Fellowship) was founded in 2010 by Debbie Thrower. www.annachaplaincy.org.uk (accessed 4th December 2024).

the more relaxed we will be about speaking to people from all sorts of ages and backgrounds. And the more we focus on Jesus rather than ourselves, the more we can retain our sense of humour and leave behind any idea of self-importance.

The questions at the end of each chapter are intended to help us explore the Bible passages that have been referred to in each chapter, our own personal growth and our ministry of 'helps', whether it's official or not. They can also be used for a regular group Bible study or life group.

Think about! *Reflections on Bible passages and your own walk with the Lord*

1. Have you ever felt the need to 'slow down' in your own life? How did you feel about it?
2. Read Hebrews 12:7-11. What has been your reaction to God's discipline in your own life?

Think about! *Your own gifts and ministry*

1. Where do you think God is leading in the way your gifts are used?
2. Is adjusting to a 'slower pace' when visiting elderly people, or those who are going through difficult experiences, a challenge for you?
3. Do you think it is helpful to consciously bring your experiences of life into your ministry, or are they a distraction?

1
God's faithfulness and ours

Recently I've been reading about the relationship between David and Jonathan in 1 Samuel. When we read this story, we often concentrate on David's role, because we know that he is going to turn out to be the famous, anointed king of Israel, but I want to look primarily at Jonathan's role and see what we can learn about faithfulness.

God's faithfulness in our early experiences

When we go through adolescence, if we are fortunate we experience the faithfulness of our family, teachers and friends. Even when we are failed by family, there are often people like youth leaders who encourage us and believe in us. We know that there are young people who have never had anyone to believe in them. What a sad state of affairs! If we meet with God at this crucial juncture of our lives, we will discover God's faithfulness to us. And then we will need the courage to take the decision to go through with the consequences of commitment to Him.

Our lives as adolescents are a bit like the story of the D-Day veterans. During the eightieth anniversary celebrations of that historic occasion, many of them said how foolish, carefree and young they were when they signed up to be involved. Until they started disembarking from the boats onto the shore, they had no idea what was in store for them. By then it was too late to go back. Due to the terrible circumstances of war, they were forced to go on.

Happily, we are not in the same circumstances as the soldiers of the Second World War, but we need great courage to go forward both at the threshold of adulthood and in times of trials, including the trials of old age.

David and Jonathan's relationship

Jonathan found himself in impossible circumstances. Although he disagreed with his father, Saul, he was faithful to him all the way through his life. He put himself out for David, as we are shown in 1 Samuel 20:4, when he says, 'Whatever you want me to do, I'll do for you.' In verse 34 it says that Jonathan was 'grieved at his father's shameful treatment of David'. But while Jonathan believed in the 'sworn friendship' he and David had together (verse 42), Jonathan stayed with his father, and even fought for him at the decisive battle of Gilboa.

Jonathan showed extraordinary faithfulness in his loyalty to his family. At the same time, he encouraged David to find 'strength in God' rather than in his glorious future (1 Samuel 23:16). Jonathan was interested in principle, not in personal gain. When in chapter 20:31, Saul pointed out that if David was victorious, Jonathan would never inherit the kingdom as Saul's son, Jonathan showed no concern, because that was not an important goal in his life. When David showed self-pity and desperation in what he said in chapter 20:1, Jonathan replied with wisdom and assurance.

Listening to those who have become disillusioned

Sadly, Christian people haven't always been as faithful to each other as Jonathan was to David. Sometimes, instead of being peace-loving and eager for reconciliation, they have been self-serving and ambitious for themselves. I have met people of all ages who have been disillusioned by quarrels they have witnessed in churches, both ones they were involved in and disagreements they have observed from the sidelines. Sometimes they have found themselves cold-shouldered by people because they appeared to back the 'wrong side'. It has caused some of them to leave the church and even give up their faith.

How important it is in these circumstances to reiterate the faithfulness of God, despite the imperfections of Christians. It takes time on the part of the pastoral visitor to listen to the details of such stories, especially when the resulting bitterness has festered over the years. Fortunately, God is still pursuing us into old age. Over a period of time, I visited a man who had been made bitter by observing church quarrels when he was younger. During one visit he was able to say the Lord's Prayer with me, and when he came to the words, 'Forgive us our sins, for we also forgive everyone who sins against us' (Luke 11:4), he started crying. God did a work of reconciliation in his heart before he passed away.

I have seen some of the leadership infighting which has gone on in various churches. Each time, whatever position I have taken, I have known that I have a conscious choice: feel upset, turn against people, refuse to talk to those who disagree with me and refuse to understand them, or consciously choose to forgive any perceived wrong and to go on building bridges. This can save us years of bitterness and barren years of not experiencing God's intimate presence in our lives.

Holding on to God's faithfulness changes us, and some people need to return to that understanding in their later years. If we minister among them, we should help them to be able to do that.

David went the extra mile. He not only honoured Saul's family after his death, but he also searched out the weakest member of the family to honour him. In 2 Samuel 9, we have the story of Mephibosheth, the disabled son of Jonathan. David went out of his way to find him. In verse 1 he asked, 'Is there anyone still left of the house of Saul to whom I can show kindness?' When we discover that, after that, Mephibosheth always ate at the king's table, we are reminded of how God is continually seeking us out, to show us kindness. As pastoral visitors who minister among the disillusioned, we should be mirroring that gratuitous kindness. David's motivation came from his experience of God's goodness to him and his deep understanding that he didn't deserve any of it.

Earlier crises in our own lives and their effect on our pastoral ministry

Being reminded of our encounters with God at key moments in our lives can help us understand what older people recall, and what younger people suffer, and it is always the experiences of crisis that help us listen to others. In later years I have been grateful for the times of crisis in my life that have helped me identify with those of others. If you listen out to the Holy Spirit, He will guide you to people with parallel or similar experiences.

Probably the most difficult experience of my life was a breakdown at the age of eighteen. 'Breakdown' is quite an old-fashioned word for what we would now call intense anxiety and depression, but in my case, 'breakdown' was an appropriate word, because suddenly I could no longer function. In fact, I took to my bed. I had no idea of the concepts of depression and anxiety, or suppressed feelings of anger or inadequacy (because such things were not discussed when I was a teenager; happily, that has changed, so that there is now a much healthier feeling of openness when discussing mental health issues). I found that I could hardly move my body. I had panic attacks which I experienced as similar to the symptoms of a heart attack. I had the scariest experiences of disassociation, which I didn't feel I could share with anyone in case people thought I was going mad. I was constantly anxious about my health and my future. I was plunged into the depths of depression. I was convinced that I was about to die, and I saw no hope for my life. I didn't want to live, and I was too scared to die.

Sometimes these unforeseen crises tie in with how God is moving in our lives, and when we look back, we can see how the two are intertwined. About six weeks before the initial episode of breakdown, I had tried talking to God honestly for the first time in many years. I had experienced a church upbringing, which made faith seem acceptable in childhood, but on the cusp of adulthood no longer made sense. In my anger and frustration about the hypocrisies and traditions of religion, I shouted to God in my head as I walked across the school playground. 'If You're there, and not a figment of someone's imagination, You'd better show me You're there, because otherwise I'm going to get on with my life and ignore You.'

I've since discovered that this can be a very 'dangerous' prayer, because if it's genuine, God has the habit of answering. Since then, I've suggested it to several people and have been amazed at what has happened as a result. One was a neighbour who, in their perplexity, started writing letters to God, just in case He should be around, and God responded to the cry of this person's heart.

Six weeks after my prayer, I was struck down by total helplessness. I'd always been a voracious reader, but suddenly I didn't want to read anything at all. I'd always wanted to sneak in as many questionable TV programmes as possible without my parents finding out. Now, the slightest reverberation of gunshot in my favourite thrillers left me shaking. The only stories which calmed me were the ones in the Gospels about Jesus. I was drawn to the Great Healer.

There followed long medical sessions, visits to the psychiatrist, medication, inability to concentrate on anything academic, and extraordinary feelings of failure. I had a four-month period of complete inactivity, a two-year period of gradual recovery and then a further four-year period of very gradual return to normality but still experiencing some symptoms.

What was behind all this emotional trauma? Certainly, there were family quarrels which had never been resolved and for which I took a responsibility that was beyond me. There were unrealistic ambitions on the part of my parents who wanted me to be 'top' all the time, which didn't tie in with my real abilities, but deeper than that were the issues I needed to face before I reached adulthood. What was the purpose of my life? In what direction was I really going? Did I have the courage to grasp the challenges of life?

Making important choices

Later, at university, I came to see that choosing to follow God or not was like the tributaries of a river, going off in different directions from each other. I had the freedom to choose which direction to go but I sensed that the choice had consequences, and I needed to face up to them. After a service when the preacher pointed this out very clearly, I went back to my hall of residence knowing that I had to make a decision. Sometime later, a speaker at a Christmas service pointed out that the wise men had been forced to go back home 'by another route' (Matthew 2:12) because they had encountered Jesus and their lives had changed.

We don't know whether a different route could have been taken in our life, and sometimes in old age we can spend time guessing about what else we could have done with our lives, but we have to choose to trust God to guide us aright.

When we look back at such trials, we can truly say with the psalmist, 'It was good for me to be afflicted so that I might learn your decrees' (Psalm 119:71).

Satisfaction or regret?

Have I ever regretted that decision to follow God? I won't give you an 'everything has been lovely as a result' quick answer. You will never understand other people's dilemmas if you assume that. Sometimes I've hung on to faith with grim determination. Other times I've railed against God's demands on my life. But most of the time

I've known it was the right decision. 'There is a way that appears to be right, but in the end it leads to death,' says Proverbs 14:12. May God protect us from that way. I have always found different songs and hymns centring on the pictures of God being a rock or an anchor to be very helpful in my hour of need, and I come back to those pictures again and again.

If you have encountered the faithfulness of God in your life, you will always be reaching back in your mind to those experiences. They are like a great big rock you cling to in the midst of life's troubles. Slowing down is an opportunity to meditate on God's faithfulness in hymns and verses of Scripture, and to look back at the deliverances in our own lives. Affirming God's faithfulness as a church can strengthen us, which is why in the Old Testament people got together on a regular basis to affirm the great stories of deliverance. It's also why church online or YouTube is so helpful to people who can't get out to church in person. They may need the next generation to help them access it on their computers, but it's a wonderful resource. It's also why the BBC's *Songs of Praise* is such a great source of encouragement to older people.

Engaging with older people who have no formal religion

There's nothing to beat a face-to-face experience in a residential home or an independent living community. Sometimes I've been to a home where there don't appear to be any religious residents, but sharing stories together has opened up the desire for a frank exchange of experiences. If, as the facilitator, you allow people the freedom to say what they want and you listen with respect without judging them, there will be times when they want to know more about God.

'Wow!' I said to one group. 'You must know each other very well to be this honest when you are sharing.'

'No, we don't,' they replied. 'We only do this when you come.'

On another occasion, out of a light-hearted Easter quiz came the story of the repentant thief on the cross and his turning to Jesus at the end of his life.[4] 'So what's all this about?' asked one lady. When I told her, she said that the hairs on the back of her neck stood up as she felt the truth of that story, and she realised that this sort of encounter could happen to her as well. It wasn't a forced, religious occasion, just a sharing time inspired by the Holy Spirit.

The choice of way opens up at different times for different people, but in my ministry among the elderly, it's quite clear that the way also opens up in old age – perhaps through isolation or loneliness, perhaps through physical weakness, or through the realisation that material goals have not been enough or that the family has let individuals down, perhaps through the terror of approaching death or the prospect of judgement when we know that we are inadequate. Whatever the reason, a deep conversation with someone in old age, about what they really feel, can have eternal results.

Nothing else can give the peace of knowing that sins are forgiven; nothing else can give the assurance that Jesus understands our weaknesses, because Jesus is the perfect high priest who can understand what we are going

---

[4] Luke 23:39-43.

through and assure us that He knows.[5] The idea of being 'saved' may sound like an outmoded religious term, but old age and emotional turmoil in earlier life teach us that we need saving by a source outside ourselves – from our mistakes and muddled understanding, and from our wrongdoing and human pitfalls.

And, knowing that our ultimate destiny is secure, old age can present us with pleasant and unexpected by-ways. Those of us who need to 'slow down', as we care for the elderly, can remind ourselves that small acts can achieve great results – a card sent to an old friend, a phone call, the gift of a DVD or CD which gives pleasure.

This morning, I set out on a path which I know well in the countryside, but then, on a whim, I followed another bridle path, which took me through a field of buttercups, then down a quiet forest path full of delicately furred beech leaves. Then, in an ordinary field, a fawn stood quietly looking at me with interest. The days of greatest weariness can be lightened by sheer beauty emanating from the most ordinary things. The aurora borealis, or northern lights, were thought to be only the experience of those who could afford to go to certain countries or have an expensive cruise. Suddenly in 2024, by a fluke of nature, they came to the ordinary inhabitants of the UK as they looked out of their windows at night, and it was free of charge! The blessings of God are given freely. It is part of our job as we 'slow down' to share them and their source with others who are struggling.

---

[5] Hebrews 2:17-18.

Think about! *Reflections on Bible passages and your own walk with the Lord*

1. How does Psalm 119:71 resonate with you? Which picture of the faithfulness of God could you use to help you in your own meditation?
2. As you read 1 Samuel 20, what can you learn from the life of Jonathan? Caught between Saul and David, was he an inevitable 'loser'?
3. Which era of your life has been the most significant in your walk with God – either through a conversion experience or through meaningful advances in your Christian life?

Think about! *Your own gifts and ministry*

1. What experiences of God's faithfulness would you be willing to share with others? Are there other experiences and trials which you would like to ring fence as private?
2. What would you say to someone who has felt disillusioned and given up the faith because of church quarrels?
3. Have you had issues with depression and/or anxiety in your own life? Could you use any of those to help others?

2

Courage

As we have seen in the last chapter, our faithfulness can be a response to God's faithfulness. Even as we worship God 'in the great congregation' (Psalm 35:18, RSV), we are inspired to trust in God's great characteristic – faithfulness. And not only should we be inspired to trust Him, but we should also make that characteristic one of our own in the way we relate to others.

Sometimes that response requires great courage on our part, especially when we have to trust in God's faithfulness through faith alone. And that requires gritting our teeth and getting on with the job. We know that the phrase 'Fear not' is a regular feature in Bible stories, so we are comforted in knowing that even the great heroes of the Old and New Testaments were prone to fear.

Gideon's background and courage

One of the characters who had to find a lot of courage was Gideon. In Judges 6 we read the beginning of his story. In verse 13, we find that he is a questioner: 'If the LORD is with us, why has all this happened to us?' Those who like to question often overthink what is happening. We look ahead and like to have all the answers in advance: 'What happens if this doesn't work out?' 'What happens if I end up looking like a fool?' 'What happens if I lose all my money?' 'How should I prepare for disaster?' 'What happens if I get this wrong and God hasn't really spoken to me?'

However, although we are called upon to have faith and courage, that does not mean we cannot ask questions. They are often questions which are worth asking. We need to face up to things which could go wrong and think about the risks we are taking. In verse 15, Gideon claims that his clan is 'the weakest in Manasseh, and I am the least in my family'. We see time and again both in the Bible and in Christian biographies that God does not care about our background. It's not just a case of promoting those who come from a working-class background (which tends to be a socially or politically fashionable position); it's a case of seeing that our social background (poor or rich; working, middle or upper class) and our ethnicity are irrelevant as to whether God wants to use us, even though our background may turn out to be useful to the ministry which God assigns us to. Just as in salvation 'there is neither Jew nor Gentile … male [or] female' (Galatians 3:28), so is that background information irrelevant to what God gives us to accomplish in our lives.

Saul was a highly educated, religious and upper-class Jew, but God had a claim on his life in just the same way as he had a plan for Mary, the mother of Jesus – someone who was very young, poor and from an obscure background. In following God's plan for our lives, we don't need to take too much notice of our inheritance. I remember the members of our Manchester Street Pastors teams who were former drug dealers or criminals. God certainly could and did use them to connect with the needy on the streets. But He also used those from a middle-class and educated background. What is important is whether we are available to God and guided by the Holy Spirit.

Gideon wants 'a sign that it is really you talking to me' (v17). That seems to be respected by the Lord, and in verse 21 we see that God does send him a miracle, confirming the authenticity of the call. It is wise to consider whether a suspected call is just part of our imagination or whether God is really speaking to us. If we ask for confirmation in a genuine spirit of wanting to follow God's will, He will show us what is right.

But this is just the beginning of Gideon's journey and, as he receives assurance from God, Gideon has to show courage, and we can learn from this ourselves. In verses 25-27 Gideon has to go against his father's worship of Baal, and Gideon's family has a strong hold on him. He obeys God and cuts down his father's altar to Baal, but he does it at night so that no one could know who has done it. I like this part of the story because it shows me something about courage. We might think that there isn't much hope for Gideon in the courage department because he can't stand up to his own family, never mind a national enemy, but we learn here about the progress of courage in our lives. Sometimes one small step takes us further in our ability to show courage, because we are encouraged by God's response to our faith, and it steels our nerves. Don't be afraid of the little steps in following God, because God always seems to reward us for taking them, even when they seem a bit pathetic.

Opposition from those we love best

It's sometimes a lot harder to stand up to our family's opposition than to the scorn of strangers. When my husband and I first went to France to do Christian work, the opposition of our parents was considerable and very hard to bear, partly because it was so emotionally charged. When we lived on a French housing estate in northern Marseille, I was glad that there were no phone connections because I found my mother crying on the other end of the phone very upsetting. I tried to write a comforting letter to her each week, and when she wrote back in critical style, I found it easier if my husband read the letter first. That made it seem one step removed and not so wounding and I coped much more easily. I should say that, years later, my mum and I were reconciled, and I realised that it was only extreme anxiety and unhappiness which drove her to that reaction.

I've known other people who have experienced opposition to full-time Christian work both from their unbelieving families and from fellow Christians. I know of a man whose family felt that he was far too well qualified and had far too many opportunities for prestigious work in the UK to justify him going to an isolated and poverty-stricken country as a full-time Christian worker. Somehow his family had not understood the parable Jesus told about the seed falling into the ground before it produces fruit.[6] He worked there for many years and said he never regretted the decision.

But Gideon had a surprise waiting for him. In verse 31, his father chose to defend him, instead of being part of the

---

[6] John 12:24.

opposition. He employed impeccable logic: 'If Baal really is a god, he can defend himself when someone breaks down his altar.' This is a lesson for us in courage. When it seems as though we will never have the courage to face the opposition, God can completely change the opposition.

The Holy Spirit in an ordinary work situation

I experienced this myself once when I was a teacher. The parent of a pupil threatened one of my colleagues and accused her of teaching a racist book. The book was part of the National Curriculum syllabus! The mother was extremely articulate and able to carry a lot of influence in the community. Her daughter, who was very popular among her peers, was enjoying the attention that her mother's outspoken attitude was giving her. I felt that I should tell my colleague to let me, as her line manager, deal with the situation, and the next time the girl was on her phone in her lesson she should send her to me.

When this happened, I decided to phone the parent before she came in. I prayed for a peaceful resolution. I spoke to the mother on the phone, and she was very angry. As the conversation continued, I asked her why she felt so angry. Suddenly, this confident woman started crying on the other end of the phone. She explained to me that so often in her life she had been the victim of racism, and she was determined that her daughter should not suffer in the same way. That was why she had reacted so instinctively to her daughter's description of the book. I asked her all about her earlier experiences of racism and said how sorry I was to hear about her sufferings. Then I said that she was welcome to come into school and to talk to me face to face, but that my colleague had not the slightest desire to show a racist attitude in class. All through the conversation I prayed.

At the end, she thanked me for my understanding. The girl in question was annoyed that she had not been the centre of an exciting drama, but she never caused my colleague any more trouble afterwards. My colleague couldn't believe the result and pushed to know how it had been achieved. The only answer I could honestly give her was prayer and the work of the Holy Spirit. She was dumbfounded but said she had read somewhere that prayer did work!

The need to keep on exercising faith and courage

Even after Gideon demonstrates a small amount of courage, he keeps on asking for reassurance from God, and God keeps on giving it to him. God seems to want to help us in the courage department. And it's just as well. In the department of faith and courage, the next time we are tested it seems just as hard as the first time. Faith will always demand courage in belief-stretching moments.

In the next chapter of Judges, we see that courage is not the same thing as boasting. In Judges 7:2-3, God tells Gideon that in appointing those who will be fighting in the army he has too many men and that 'Israel would boast against me, "My own strength has saved me."' So God says that 'anyone who trembles with fear may turn back'. That reassures me that even when I haven't continued doing something through fear, God understands. If you've made a few U-turns in following God in your life, it is wonderful that you can know that too.

Gideon is still fearful at this point, but God helps him. 'If you are afraid to attack, go down to the camp … and listen' (vv10-11). 'Afterwards, you will be encouraged' (v11). God allows us many opportunities to be encouraged. I'm sure there were a lot of stalwart fighters in Israel who were ready to lose their lives in battle. Gideon wasn't one of those (he wasn't a David or a Samson), but God took him through each step of the assignment, and He will take us through those impossible circumstances which need impossible courage, even if we are very weak.

The Bible tells us in Judges 7:15 that when Gideon hears what is happening in the Midianite camp, he worships God. Godly courage will always make us worship God rather than think how wonderful we are.

In the next chapter, we hear that Gideon is able to offer diplomacy as well. In Judges 8:1 we hear that the Ephraimites, who were part of a closely related tribe, challenge him 'vigorously', but Gideon knows how to deal with them. 'At this, their resentment against him subsided' (v3).

After he has again led the fighting against the enemy, his men ask him to become the national leader, but Gideon is very clear in his response: 'The LORD will rule over you' (v23). Gideon knows his limitations. His courage is for a special crisis, and he never tries to take credit for it.

Because this is a record of God's dealings with human beings, and not a fairy story, we know that Gideon is finally tempted by money, and this leads him into idolatry. An experience of great courage and reliance on the Lord does not mean we will never go astray. Each step of our journey, continuing into old age, means we have to rely on God and trust in Him for courage to be obedient each time afresh.

Different types of courage

I have always admired physical courage because it is not one of my strong points. One of my children chose to do a three months' adventure course in Austria, which involved crossing a glacier in the middle of the night while being roped to a team of people, and going potholing. I knew that she had hated potholing when she tried it at school.

'Are you sure you want to do it?' I asked her.

'Yes,' she replied. 'I want to overcome my fears.'

'Could this person be related to me?' I asked myself. I am afraid of heights, and I could not imagine myself taking part in a physical adventure which involved scaling heights on a cliff edge. Fortunately, God has never asked me to achieve physical feats for which I need courage. Every time I read about physical courage in others, I feel full of admiration.

But there are other types of courage which God has asked me to face up to. One was the discovery in my thirties, after two episodes of adult measles and hepatitis and two pregnancies and births very close together, that I had become seriously deaf. I remember the night when I knew it had happened. It seemed that I was awake all night, grieving over my lost hearing and wondering how I was ever going to manage a job as a teacher of teenage children. It was likely to ruin my career and the possibility of earning any money to support our family and help our children. I spent the night feeling the blackness of despair and the feeling that God had completely deserted me.

I slept briefly for a couple of hours after dawn. When I woke again, I knew that I could not afford any self-pity. I felt God speaking to me: 'You've wallowed in self-pity for the last few hours and the time has come to put that aside, because it won't help you at all. I've allowed this to happen. I have a plan for your life, and you need to find practical solutions.' The knowledge that God is intervening in our lives gives us courage.

That hasn't been the only time that I have needed courage to overcome the disaster of deafness. The sense of frustration and the desire to give up has happened again and again. But since that night, I've never allowed it to defeat me completely. 'Ah,' commented the audiologist, when I was tested for deafness and shown the need to wear hearing aids. 'You are so deaf that if a jumbo jet were to take off in the room next to us, you couldn't hear!' Because I felt the presence of God in this situation, I could actually laugh about this comment.

How do you cope in a noisy classroom, when you know you will not be able to distinguish individual questions? The answer is perfect classroom management and discipline. 'It is rude to be talking when someone else is asking a question,' I assured my pupils. I never told them that I couldn't hear, only that their behaviour needed to be better. And they never complained about my discipline.

'How come Mum can never hear anything,' one of my children commented in the back of the car, 'unless you say something rude and then she immediately picks it up?' Oh! the magic of a mother's all-knowingness!

The positive value of our trials

Apart from the opportunity to show courage and determination, has this affliction ever proved useful? Many times! When I first ministered in Salford among people from deprived backgrounds, I met so many people with bad hearing. When I have visited care homes as a chaplain, I have met many old people with hearing problems who are feeling hopeless and frustrated. The first thing I do is take out the hearing aids from my ears and show them. 'Look,' I say, 'I've been wearing these for the last thirty years. I have worn them when I have taught teenagers in a noisy comprehensive school. If I can do that and survive, so can you.'

One observation which old people who have recently started wearing hearing aids often make is that they've spent a lot of money on these aids and they don't make any difference. 'That's how it feels to begin with,' I commiserate with them. 'But gradually your brain adapts. It's worth it if you stick at it.'

Being deaf in the long term also helps me know how to talk to older people one to one in the clearest voice possible. This has nothing to do with loudness of voice; it has everything to do with clear enunciation. You can phase out the speech of background speakers and learn to concentrate on the speaker who is near you. You can learn to lipread, even without attending special lessons.

Paul said that he had been given a thorn in the flesh. 'Three times I pleaded with the Lord to take it away from me. But he said to me, "My grace is sufficient for you, for my power is made perfect in weakness"' (2 Corinthians 12:8-9).

Watching your own child suffer

One of the times when you need great courage is when one of your own children is suffering. I can't imagine how it feels to watch a child suffer with cancer, but I do know how it feels to watch your teenager go through terrible depression. As I have explained above, the experience of having a breakdown involving depression, anxiety and a sense of disassociation is a living hell. But the experience of watching a loved child go through the same thing when she is fourteen years of age is twice the amount of hell. You wonder whether you are partly to blame – have you been a bad parent? You wonder whether your own experience of depression means that she inherited genes that predisposed her to that terrible experience.

You need courage in a different way than you need it when you are having the experience of depression yourself. You have to show that you believe in the child who is suffering, that there will be an end in sight and that they can be successful in their lives despite this. You have to have the courage to tell them that they can be with you whenever they want to be, day or night. I can remember the times when I needed to rely on God so much that however tired I was or however much work was accumulating, I needed to read God's Word each night in order to get through my own reaction to the crisis.

You need courage and conviction when you feel that professional advice is wrong. In the case of our daughter, we went to see a psychiatrist privately in order to hurry up any available treatment. I was unhappy with her advice because it seemed inappropriate for the personality of our daughter – not the medical prescription, but the advice to join other troubled adolescents at the private hospital where the psychiatrist practised – and not just because of the cost involved. Our daughter pleaded not to be sent there because she wanted to stay with her family (one of our other daughters was the only person who could even raise the glimmer of a smile on her face). Would the company of other troubled adolescents be any better than this, we wondered?

The consultant also told her to her face that she would never be successful in a profession and would always have problems with depression – not something a fourteen-year-old or her parents want to hear! As a result of that consultation, we were fast-tracked to the NHS hospital consultant. Even as he prescribed a regime of medication and CBT,[7] he assured us that it was the best thing for her to stay with her family. He also told her that although it was a serious illness, she would eventually recover and be successful. He was right! Four years later, she applied for medicine (to begin with she just wanted to leave school at sixteen, which we were happy for her to do) and has become a happy and fulfilled GP.

It takes courage to believe in God's promises, especially when it involves someone in your family. Psalm 116:3-4 tells us about this experience.

> I was overcome by distress and sorrow.
> Then I called on the name of the LORD:
> 'LORD, save me!'

The assurance that the Lord has heard comes in verse 7:

> Be at rest once more, O my soul,
> for the LORD has been good to you.
> (NIV 1984)

---

[7] Cognitive behavioural therapy.

Courage as we face old age

Just as people need courage to make life-changing decisions on the cusp of adulthood, as they approach old age they also need courage, and in our role as visitor or minister, we may be crucial in helping people to find.

One of the most difficult decisions older people have to make is when or if to move out of the family home. For the younger generation it seems like a straightforward, practical decision. For the elderly, it is a case of, 'How am I going to do away with all my memories of a former life, when I brought up my children, when every room speaks of a treasured happiness?' I remember a lady in her nineties, whom I met in a unit of sheltered housing. She had been fortunate enough to move into sheltered accommodation on the same road as she had lived all her life. But she wept inconsolably as she told me about her former house and garden. By moving away from it, she felt she was negating the whole purpose of her life.

If the elderly person is a Christian, it may still be a difficult decision emotionally, but there is a strong sense of no home being a permanent one because they are 'looking for the city that is to come' (Hebrews 13:14). 'I wish I had come much earlier,' a new resident told me. She knew she had a ministry among her fellow retirees. 'And I wish my husband had not spent so long trying to resurrect an old denominational church to keep it from closing.' To those who pine after keeping their church buildings going at all costs, take note!

A Christian visitor can help in difficult circumstances

Then there is the courage to face up to difficult medical needs, and doctors who have less time than they used to.

A lady in one of my parishes suddenly developed Parkinson's disease after a challenging family experience. At first she was prescribed medication which stopped the shaking, but then suddenly a new doctor in the nearby hospital clinic decided it was not good for her heart and substituted another medicine, which did not help her in the same way. Week after week she tried to ring the hospital department and the GP to talk to them about it, but no one listened, and the unhelpful medication was prescribed yet again. She was upset and frustrated and felt as if no one understood. She needed extraordinary courage not to give up.

In those circumstances, can a Christian visitor help? I believe they can. They can't alter medication prescriptions, but they can make phone calls and accompany someone to a medical appointment and act as an advocate. A Christian cannot (and should not) do everything. But they can do something. And for an older person who has no family around them, this can mean so much – knowing that someone cares for them and believes in them.

So much of such work will not be known by anyone else. But it will be known to God. I always find Hebrews 6:10 an encouragement as I have practised the gift of 'helps': 'God is not unjust; he will not forget your work and the love you have shown him as you have helped his people and continue to help them.'

Trying to negotiate phone calls when you are too deaf to hear what is being said, when you have forgotten passwords and pin numbers which will give you access to your account, is very upsetting. Yes, a younger family member can help if you are fortunate enough to have someone like that, but they often don't have the time to spare. It needs the strength of God to sustain you in these circumstances.

The role of carer needs great courage

Being a full-time carer for someone who has dementia is hugely draining, whether the person is a parent, a spouse or a sibling. Each variety of dementia makes different demands on loved ones, and a visitor should never assume what the demands are. They should ask and listen carefully to the reply.

In my own situation, I haven't felt the need to reply sixteen times to the same question too hard, but I have found the lack of intellectual stimulation very difficult, because so much of the day is spent getting through ordinary, mundane tasks which require no brain work. If your partner, parent or sibling can't walk and doesn't want to be separated from you, you are stuck in your house like a prison. If the person you are looking after becomes dogmatic and critical, the stress is enormous, because the temptation to answer back and provoke a quarrel is overwhelming. If your partner has a physical accident and can't move and becomes even more confused, you may well be expected to nurse them without any back-up, and it is exhausting. If your partner refuses to socialise so that people forget about you, then you will live in a very lonely world. I know people suffering in each of these categories. The burden they carry at times seems intolerable. A phone call or a timely visit makes all the difference. It is very easy for members of a busy church to forget about these carers.

Courage to give you resilience in difficult circumstances

Charities are aware of this strain and try their best to support, but no one can be there all the time. Carers need extraordinary resilience to survive, and it is only God who can give you that resilience. 'God has not given us a spirit of fear, but of power and of love and of a sound mind,' writes the apostle in 2 Timothy 1:7 (NKJV). Refusing to indulge in self-pity and believing that God has a purpose for you in these most difficult of circumstances are essential principles if you are going to survive the test of being a long-term carer.

'Slow down' while being a full-time carer? I should say so! Slow down when you are still mentally and physically active? Slow down when you yourself are elderly and struggling? It's only God who can give you the ability to endure with courage.

In an age of 'tell all', when people who routinely expose those who have hurt them or made their lives difficult, God still calls us to be faithful. David had plenty of opportunities to hit back at Saul and his family, but David relied on God's good purposes for him rather than on easy jibes and self-pity. We are called to do the same, and it is not an easy path to follow, especially when other people cannot see into the depths of our experiences.

If you are a carer for someone with dementia, it will not only be heartbreaking if they become violent or display characteristics that are different from how they were when well, but their tendencies and characteristics, which are often exaggerated by the illness, may remind us of the times they have annoyed us in the past. It is so easy to polarise your past experience of marriage. You may think that you have had the perfect marriage or family relationship in the past, and so, while heartbroken, do all out of love or, at the opposite extreme, in anger and frustration leave the dementia sufferer to the sole care of professionals because you cannot cope any more. In my professional experience I have seen both happen.

'I would do it all again for love and to keep him here longer,' pined one of my residents after the death of their spouse.

'Don't expect me to be your personal nurse,' announced another person to their partner, who was a resident in a home I was visiting. 'I have no intention of giving my retirement years to your inadequacies.'

We should not scorn the last response too quickly, especially if we have not suffered in the same way. It takes superhuman effort not to be resentful or illogically angry, or even not to feel somewhere deep down that your partner or family member has succumbed to illness on purpose in order to make your life difficult.

How can I find God's plan when life is so hard?

The question I regularly ask myself in the midst of restrictions is, 'How can I fulfil God's calling to me now in these less-than-ideal circumstances?' In a recent *Songs of Praise* episode,[8] celebrating the ministry of carers, one woman who looked after her seriously ill husband and son for years said that after she had started the day by herself, lighting a candle as a prayer, she was inspired to write her

---

[8] *Songs of Praise*, 9th June 2024, celebrating carers in Norfolk. Available on BBC iPlayer, www.bbc.co.uk/programmes/m00204cp (accessed 4th December 2024).

own prayer and a verse of Scripture, which she then sent to two hundred people. Many people were encouraged by her ministry, and she did it all without stepping outside her own front door. As her vicar said, she reached more people like that than he did through his weekly sermon.

A couple at Christ Church, Downend, Bristol, who support our community outreach, Vintage Adventure, tell the health workers and neighbours about this monthly event. They draw other needy people into our church community through their testimony, despite the illness that forces them to largely stay at home.

Ministering from a position of weakness is always powerful. 'No one can understand what it's like,' shares my friend, 'unless they are doing it themselves.'

Visiting and helping from a position of weakness

In our ministry to older people, we should try to share their burdens. As a couple where one of us has Alzheimer's and the other is the full-time carer, we find visiting other couples in a similar situation brings encouragement and helps us to use our gifts. We can also offer couples a safe place in our churches so that the carers can have a break, even when they stay under the same roof. Each partner in the couple can talk to other people, do different activities and just be in a different environment. In our church we offer this through Vintage Adventure and through a dementia café.

Jesus said that when we visit someone in prison, we are visiting Him.[9] Many carers are living in a prison, unable to leave the house, unable to leave a 'clingy' partner with

---

[9] Matthew 25:36-40.

anyone else. As Christians we can offer this small act of love.

Professional help and down-to-earth love

And what happens when there are past resentments, or even past abuse? As someone who offers the gift of 'helps' we may be out of our depth on this one and it is time to signpost people to experts. Admiral nurses are particularly skilled in listening to the stories of carers, and we should take advantage of their services.[10] Long years of resentment can build up, and we need to be able to share that resentment with someone else who is trained and experienced in giving guidance. Maybe our churches should make sure that someone is trained for this task, or at least have a list of trained counsellors who can help.

But on a less intense level, there may be much that an ordinary Christian friend or visitor can do to relieve the burden. 'Caring' is not a glamorous job. In fact, it is often hidden. I know someone who regularly has to change the catheter for their parents and suffers their complaints and grumbles rather than their appreciation. Many spouses have to look after incontinent partners. Yes, there are official carers who visit (thank goodness), but inevitably family members will end up doing difficult tasks. A phone call from someone outside the situation can make someone feel remembered and loved. A call or a message that says, 'I've just been praying for you, and I wondered how you were getting on,' lifts the spirit in an otherwise bleak day.

---

[10] www.dementiauk.org/information-and-support/how-we-can-support-you/what-is-an-admiral-nurse (accessed 4th December 2024).

Slow down for an individual caregiver? I should say so! If you are someone who needs intellectual stimulus, where do you get it from? TV? Telephone calls? The internet? Emails? Books? Podcasts? It may be vital to factor such things into your day. A friend was asked by his wife, who suffered from vascular dementia, to go to bed in the early evening with her and never to let go of her hand so she didn't feel so afraid. That's a tall order for someone who does not need the same amount of sleep. He solved it by wearing headphones and listening to worship music and cricket commentaries as he held her hand. Such an action takes a huge amount of loving commitment and faithfulness. And how about social interaction that has nothing to do with dementia? Those of us who are full-time carers have to believe that God knows exactly what our needs are. One day we 'shall know ... even as [we are now] fully known' (1 Corinthians 13:12). God understands the complexities and vagaries of our personality right now. And one day we will understand why we have passed through this time of trial and sadness. One day we will come face to face with Jesus, and God will wipe 'every tear' from our eyes (Revelation 7:17).

Hebrews 12:2-3 says:

> Let us fix our eyes on Jesus, the author and
> perfecter of our faith, who for the joy set before
> him endured the cross, scorning its shame, and sat
> down at the right hand of the throne of God.
> Consider him who endured such opposition from
> sinful men, so that you will not grow weary and
> lose heart.
> (NIV 1984)

Jesus showed extraordinary courage in following His calling because He knew that, through the cross, He would achieve lasting salvation for us, and that He would again be reunited with His Father in heaven, for ever. We can choose to be courageous in supporting our parents or our partners with dementia because we know that one day we will be reunited in heaven and we will hear the words, 'Well *done*, good and faithful servant … Enter into the joy of your lord' (Matthew 25:23, NKJV).

Think about! *Reflections on Bible passages and your own walk with the Lord*

1. Who else can you think of in the Bible, in addition to Gideon, who needed a sign that it was really God who was speaking to them?
2. In what ways do you feel encouraged by Bible characters who needed assurance from God when they were not feeling courageous?
3. In what ways have you proved 2 Corinthians 12:9 to be true in your own life?

Think about! *Your own gifts and ministry*

1. Have you been able to use your own struggles with courage to reassure someone you are visiting?
2. What different types of courage do you find difficult or easy in your own life?
3. How would you help someone who feels that they have let God down badly in a decision they have made through either disobedience or weakness?

3
Contentment

We can believe that God has a particular job for us to do or a role to fulfil, because the Bible reassures us that He has been involved in our lives even before we were born. As David talks about God knowing every single part of our lives, he writes in Psalm 139:16, 'All the days ordained for me were written in your book before one of them came to be.' A conviction of the truth of this verse helps us to be truly content, because we know that the circumstances of our lives are not chance. We are in a particular situation because the Lord has allowed us to be there.

Contentment and selfish greed contrasted

In the Bible there are quite a few stories involving contrasting characters – those who are content with the position God has put them in, and those who are trying to do better than others for their own selfish ends, even if that means doing what is wrong. In 2 Kings 5:2 we meet a young girl from Israel who has been forced to become a slave in Aram. Instead of complaining (and no doubt she would feel like complaining in that situation!), she is so trusted that her mistress confides in her about her husband's problems, and she is able to pass on advice. Instead of wanting retribution against the enemy who has captured her, she wants to see Naaman, the commander of the army, helped and blessed: 'If only my master would see the prophet who is in Samaria! He would cure him of his leprosy' (2 Kings 5:3).

We don't hear about the girl again, but the message gets through to Naaman. As a result, Elisha is the man of God in the situation, and Naaman learns about God's greatness: 'Now I know that there is no God in all the world except in Israel' (v15). He also learns about the way God blesses His people, by giving His gifts freely.

Looking at another character in the story, Naaman was outraged that he was given what he saw as a belittling command to wash seven times in the River Jordan. 'So he turned and went off in a rage' (2 Kings 5:12). Pride and rage are the opposites of contentment. You can't do them at the same time. Fortunately, Naaman learnt from his mistakes and was healed and came to a knowledge of the true God.

Gehazi, Elisha's servant, an Israelite, is angry at the way Elisha refuses to profit from Naaman, an enemy of his people, and it leads him to become covetous, to steal and to lie. If only he were content to serve the prophet and rejoice in what has happened to Naaman, he would not suffer from leprosy for the rest of his life. This is truly a serious consequence of a lack of contentment with the position that God has given to Gehazi.

An exciting and challenging life under God's guidance

In contrast, Esther was equally content to be the niece of Mordecai as she was to be the favourite of the king. Esther 2:20 tells us, 'She continued to follow Mordecai's instructions as she had done when he was bringing her up.' However, contentment did not stop her doing something very courageous in challenging the king about his treatment of the Jews. Contentment doesn't necessarily mean an easy or a boring life! Nor did her courage prevent her from believing in prayer and fasting. She not only prayed and fasted herself but asked others to follow her in this, because she believed she needed God's extraordinary strength to resolve the situation.

Contentment isn't just an easy feeling of wellbeing or lack of expectations. It involves accepting challenges and self-sacrificial prayer. Esther was up against a man who was full of hatred, greed and ambition – Haman – and, humanly speaking, she didn't stand a chance in the contest, but with her total trust in God, she succeeded. 'Maybe you have been chosen for such a time as this,' suggests her uncle (Esther 4:14, paraphrased), and he was proved right.

Questioning God

Contentment does not mean we cannot question God and object to what we see as being unfair. I've always enjoyed walking on the moors and in the hills. When I was a vicar and lived near the Pennines, I would often walk on the Pennine Way on my day off. My face would be set against the strong wind, with my boots frequently getting stuck in the never-ending bogs, and at the same time I would be reviewing what was going on in my ministry. Sometimes I would pray for a particular person in need; sometimes I would review a meeting which had not been easy, and I would consider whether I could have reacted better or led it differently. Sometimes I was upset with God over something that had happened in my personal life. So, there, on the lonely path, I would question and sometimes shout at God. What did He think He was doing to allow these circumstances to take place?

I would also stop at a special viewpoint or a place to have my sandwich lunch and just survey the scene, internally and externally. I felt I was walking with God in all seasons. I said whatever came into my head and I reckoned God could cope with all my attitudes and moods. On occasions I would need to turn my attention to negotiate a tricky moment on the path, or jump over a stream, or gracefully finish a skid on an icy stone without breaking a bone. Several times in the winter I would find myself high up in the snow. Other walkers weren't quite as hardy or desperate as I was, so I often had the countryside to myself, apart from some startled sheep who were surprised to see me but who didn't mind me talking out loud to God. Then there were the farms to negotiate – a few dogs barking in the yard and once some cattle who raced over to me as I crossed the field. It was only when I leaped over a five-bar gate to get out of their range that I saw the notice on the other side: 'Beware the bull!'

Was I content? I wasn't peaceful, and like a lippy teenager I had far too much to say back to God, but after my day out on the moors I always felt better, and some of my emotional reactions and worries seemed to have disappeared in the driving rain.

Being honest with God

Some of us aren't naturally content. We have too many questions and arguments going on in our minds. The secret for me, as a naturally argumentative person, was to speak out my anger to God. If you have a questioning or rebellious nature, it doesn't work if you ignore your feelings or try to assume some sort of holy glow. It does help if you spread out your feelings before God. Sometimes it is even in the speaking out of the problems that we reach a resolution.

I love the story of Hezekiah, told in Isaiah 36–37 and 2 Kings 18–19. After telling the attackers of Jerusalem not to discourage his people, he received a letter from the messengers of Assyria. All the points the enemy made were logical and they were likely to cause Hezekiah big problems. When he didn't know what to do, he went up to the temple and 'spread [the letter] out before the LORD' (Isaiah 37:14). He worshipped and praised God to begin with (an action of faith saying that God was greater than his enemy), and then, acknowledging the truth of the threat, he pleaded with God for deliverance. Likewise, prayer for us should involve worship and spreading the problem out in detail before the Lord and pleading for His answers.

Enforced slowdowns

Over the years, I've had many opportunities in ministry and in everyday life to explore contentment, which is not naturally part of my character. When my husband bought a caravan on a small campsite in France so we would always have somewhere to go on annual leave away from the demands of the parish, I found myself asking, 'What am I going to do there?'

One of the answers was to get a bike to explore the bike paths. I'd never really cycled since marriage, but all these paths seemed to beckon – through the forests, down to the beach or into the town for coffee. I started noticing herons on the riverbank and how people were improving their allotments each year. Contentment came from celebrating the small details of life. Everything happened in slow motion, including eating out on the decking. There was no internet connection so I couldn't solve the problems of my parishioners.

When I returned home after two weeks, the churchwardens assured me that they had loved me going away because they felt they had had a holiday too! What?! They didn't miss me? Apparently not! If I had felt driven to organise outreaches and social events, then so had they! There seemed to be a lot more contentment around when I wasn't there to organise everyone.

I don't think any of us really realised what a change of pace meant until we all went into lockdown during the Covid pandemic. On the one hand, I was working from my home office every single day, including constant telephone calls and Zoom conferences. On the other hand, there was time for mid-morning coffee on the decking, and at night a Zoom session with the family. And time to watch the news, which I had never done before. Even the Bible study home group seemed easier because you could sink into your own armchair, and it didn't matter if you slouched. And after the Bible study, there was always time to read a book or watch a TV programme.

But it was the daily one-hour walks I valued most. I found local walks and parks which I hadn't known existed before. Every walk felt like an adventure. I now knew all the winding paths through Conham Woods down to the River Avon and how many ducklings were following their mother on Magpie Bottom Pond. The small details of my surroundings were a wonderful contrast to the figures of how many people were on ventilators. People in church told me about the details of their lives too. As we had moved house fairly recently, my husband found lots of old photos to put in frames on the walls and we could discuss the memories of each photo.

Godliness and adventure

So, what does contentment mean? Does it mean an eternal lockdown when you can opt out of life's responsibilities? In 1 Timothy 6:6 Paul says that 'godliness with contentment is great gain'. So contentment must always be linked to godliness in our lives, and Paul does show that material satisfaction is not enough by itself to give us a spiritually fulfilling life. He says in verse 10 that 'the love of money is a root of all kinds of evil'. You can have love of money whether you are rich or poor, as we found out when living in North Africa. People who were very poor were always hoping that the latest influx of washing machines would solve their problems, even when there wasn't enough water to make them work. Nor does it mean that we should have no aspirations in life. Godliness isn't just about living on a hyper-spiritual plateau, where you are happy to enjoy mystical experiences halfway up a mountain, nor does it mean frequently being part of three-hour prayer meetings.

If you're going to be godly in an ungodly world, there are going to be some fights ahead, so it's not a boring life after all. And if you're going to be part of the kingdom of God, you might be taking part in a few risky adventures. If you want to read about people who have had similar adventures because they wanted to follow God, then there are plenty to start with – how about C T Studd and Gladys Aylward?[11] And you don't have to be an 'old-fashioned' missionary. What about Christians who are working on the environment in A Rocha or are involved in aid projects through Christian Aid or Tearfund?[12] Or those involved in emergency relief teams? I know a committed Christian who goes out to disaster areas with his paramedic team. Not much chance of boredom there!

Contentment doesn't mean you have to live in a rose-decorated cottage and bake your own bread. And in a society where there are so many opportunities for women, you can combine being a mother and homemaker with being a world-class scientist, astronomer or playwright, or many other things.

Is happiness our main aim in life?

A lot of people say that as long as they are happy, that is all they desire, but I've always been a bit cynical about this statement. What happens if you are satisfied with very little or have no aspirations to excel? I return to the potentially toxic word 'ambition' later in this book, but clearly some people have more ambition than others. And

---

[11] C T Studd (1860–1931) was an English missionary in China and Africa. Gladys Aylward (1902–70) was an English missionary in China.

[12] Founded in 1983, A Rocha is a Christian charity caring for the environment, www.arocha.org.uk (accessed 4th December 2024). Founded in 1945, Christian Aid is a Christian charity relieving poverty worldwide, www.christianaid.org.uk (accessed 4th December 2024). Founded in 1968 by George Hoffman, Tearfund is a Christian charity relieving poverty worldwide, www.tearfund.org (accessed 4th December 2024).

some people are wise because they reject the ambition that is going to take them away from a job they do well and is fulfilling. My son-in-law loves response policing, and he is good with people on the streets, but if he moves up too high in the establishment he will move away from people on the streets and spend more time on paperwork in the office. My husband decided not to aim to be a full-time head teacher, because he knew that he was better in the classroom and hated meetings with the council and education hierarchy.

But you could be 'indoctrinated' to believe that living in your semi-detached house, washing your car on Sunday mornings and playing golf on Saturday afternoons is enough to give you satisfaction. People cried when Stalin died. He had killed millions of people and did not allow anyone to think for themselves, and yet people who had always done what the regime told them and had not suffered persecution were happy to be under his rule and felt grief when their hero died.

It's great to have a level of satisfaction because you have enough to eat and see your children better themselves, but what about a love of freedom and a desire to think more deeply and to wonder about the purpose of life? Mother Teresa felt fulfilled because she had done what God wanted her to do, but living among the poor didn't give her an easy life.[13]

---

[13] Mother Teresa (1910–97) was an Albanian–Indian Catholic nun who worked among the poor in India.

Not necessarily an easy life

If you become a church leader, then you will know that criticism is going to be an inevitable part of what you suffer. I know pastors who after every sermon receive emails telling them how they could have taught better. If you're going to lead real people rather than robots, it's going to be challenging. Not much contentment when you try to 'knock heads together' in the PCC or bring together people who have been quarrelling for years.

Looking back at my younger self, I realise that what I most feared was mediocrity. I despised my girlfriends who just wanted to settle down and get married. Not many young people seem to make that choice of early marriage today, but of course it is an instinct to settle down and have your own family. In our world there are many young women who pursue a career or sporting achievement before they settle down. At the 2024 Paris Olympics, we heard that for the first time nurseries were provided for competitors who took their young children with them. And there is far more opportunity for MPs to breastfeed their children in Parliament and return home for bedtime. This is all to the good, and Christian couples can benefit from these arrangements too. But it's never going to be easy for a Christian single person to be godly, especially with the demands of celibacy, and loneliness, which can be very hard. Anyone in our churches of either sex who is pursuing a great career in the arts, sport or professional life needs our supportive prayers.

You can choose to delay having children, as my husband and I did, because it was easier to be involved in a church-planting team in Marseille without them. Others find out that they can't have children, and that is both an opportunity for service and a grief at the same time. I now have two daughters who have moved to very challenging situations in Central Asia along with husbands and young children. People will feel God leading them differently, and there will inevitably be self-sacrifice involved.

Challenges as we follow God

One of my colleagues in the Church of England sold his house, used the money to go to Bible school and then went off to minister in a primitive situation in Nepal along with his wife and two young children. He rode his motorbike in the Himalayas for pastoral visiting alongside his diagnostic laboratory work. Not for the faint-hearted! And after returning to the UK to allow his children to finish their education and choosing to work in a socially deprived area of Manchester as a community worker, he and his wife later went back to Nepal to work with children and offer counselling to families. For such people, taking risks for the sake of the kingdom of God gives them contentment.

Older people with greater life expectancy can go out to difficult places to do God's work. A couple in our church go out regularly to Uganda to help build schools and encourage churches there. They use their organisational skills, gained from their previous secular employment, to do something worthwhile, and as they have their pensions, they are financially self-sufficient. No sitting back and pruning the roses or going on luxury cruises for them! And I know a man in his eighties who goes out alone to kayak and camp in the Scottish lochs as well as completing walking and camping challenges in order to raise money for various charities. We should never assume that people cannot contribute to our church life when they are old. Contentment must mean more than sitting at home and twiddling our thumbs.

You can, of course, be involved in a very ordinary job, know contentment and be inspired by what you are doing. Recently on the news came the story of how a bus driver composed a song that recorded how wonderful his job was.[14] If that man spoke to his passengers in a kindly way and helped them, it would certainly have brought him contentment. Through my job as a chaplain, I have met many care workers who are delighted that they can bring help to their residents and reassure the families at the same time. A manager of a care home told me that he had originally come to do occasional handiwork at a home during his university holidays, but he had been so inspired by the devotion of the care staff there that he had decided to go back into a management training scheme after university. When I saw him stay up all night with a lonely old man who had no family and who was dying, I saw how satisfying his job was. Glamour? No. Good pay? No. Contentment, yes.

Serving God in the workplace

Welcoming people into the kingdom of God is one of the most satisfying and surprising roles of all – to find that through your prayers and conversation, someone has drawn nearer to God to find forgiveness and a new life. You can often meet more people who are searching for

---

[14] www.bbc.co.uk/news/av/uk-england-birmingham-64233461 (accessed 4th December 2024).

God in a secular workplace than you can as an official minister. It all depends what God has called you to do and when. Happily, you can use your skills in the workplace and tell others about Jesus very effectively. When I was a teacher, I had to follow rules about not proselytising in lesson time, but lots of students and teachers came to ask me about my faith after official school time was over. When we lived in Essex, I taught at a sixth-form college, which was just up the road from our church where there was a large youth group. Through my job I had lots of ready-made contacts with those who came there.

My son-in-law, who had been a highly respected engineer in London for nearly twenty years, decided to move abroad with his family in order to help the church there. He said that his colleagues were so amazed at his countercultural choice (going against ambition, financial security and ease of lifestyle) that they listened in amazement to his explanation of faith at his leaving party. These moments make an impression on those who only know about the values of this world.

You can do some very exciting things alongside your secular job. We were inspired by a couple in one of the first churches we went to in the south of England, who regularly opened their home to young people. They ran a business, but their lives were given over to inspiring young people to follow God. We worked with them in opening our own home up to the same ministry, and when we moved to north Manchester, inspired by their example, we were able to again open our home up to a non-denominational youth group on Friday evenings. Most of the young people came from backgrounds where there was no faith, but they all said how they felt at ease to be themselves and share their problems in our house. We had a special prayer room where they could talk to us about their worries, and of course we played snooker with them, watched TV and drank cola and coffee. They said they felt loved.

Such love originates in the love of the Lord Jesus, and we know from the Gospels that His life was anything but boring. Nancy, one of the older leaders who had worked with young people for many years and had spent her life before she was married as a PE teacher, saw her youth work with Urban Saints as her 'missionary' work.[15] And it was. Several people of my own age had become Christians through her testimony and, as a result, they became agents of light as teachers and youth workers themselves. I knew at least one full-time vicar who had started off as an unbelieving boyfriend of a girl who became a Christian through Nancy. The influence had spread.

When I worked as a Street Pastor in north Manchester, many of our team members had ordinary jobs. It didn't stop them knowing how to manage some very dramatic and violent incidents on the streets of the city. The salt Jesus talked about in Matthew 5 was definitely being spread out there. They weren't full-time social workers or drug advisors, but they were trained for their work and they gave up their time freely to have an influence through the church on the street. I cannot tell you the number of times a group in a bar would start heckling us because they thought we were the 'God squad'. When we explained that we were there to care for the depressed, confused and victims of abuse, and not to preach, they

---

[15] www.urbansaints.org (accessed 4th December 2024).

immediately wanted to know why we were doing this work. We explained that the love of God was our motivation, and when they found out that we paid for our own training and were working across several different church denominations, they asked us questions about faith and listened to the answers with respect. What an amazing combination of being involved with the night-time economy of our cities and the chance to tell people about Jesus.

God's calling brings contentment

God gives everyone a different calling. I didn't anticipate being called by God to work as a full-time stipendiary vicar, but it happened. Influenced by the cultural Christian background of the 1970s, I had assumed that it would be my husband who would be called to such a role. But I was wrong. It was a very clear call to me, and I relished (most of the time!) all the opportunities it presented. My husband felt called to be a full-time secondary school teacher and part-time youth worker. His love for young people and his patience in listening to them encouraged teenagers from vulnerable backgrounds to come to our house on a Friday evening. They called him 'Jesus man'. What greater compliment can you have?

Contentment doesn't mean you have to pack more and more things into your schedule. If you try to do that, you will feel more stressed and pressurised and have no opportunity to spend quality time with God. Some people have more energy than others, but there is a difference between having the energy to be busy and being constantly active because you are keyed up by anxious thoughts. That's why 'Slow down!' can be an important command to any of us at any age.

Balancing life's demands as we follow Jesus

This doesn't mean you can't have an influential job or even a lot of money as a Christian, but it does mean that it can't be the whole aim of your life. Instead of 'collateral damage', we might think of money and influence as 'collateral advantage', but we have to be sure we can hold them lightly. If you are skilled in your job and get a promotion, you are likely to be content. If your career ladder climbing takes precedence over caring for your family or following God, then you are likely to be unhappy. If you are given more money than you need, then it is your responsibility to use it well.

In Salford, there was a group of anonymous Christian businessmen who funded something called 'Seedbed'. They provided starter funds for Christians who had good ideas for helping others and they were advised by Christians who knew the area well. I was helped by that fund in a couple of projects. What an excellent way of doing things!

The demands of a balanced life for dual parents and one-parent families

Men and women who are high-fliers need to ask themselves whether they are being driven or whether they are called by God to have a fulfilling life. People are called to 'go slow' when they find themselves in the midst of family crises and unexpected illnesses. Such crises can cause us to ask ourselves what the real purpose of life is. It is so easy to be pulled into a perpetually crazy vortex because two people are working very long hours and have no time for each other or for their children. As Christians, whether male or female, we are called upon to earn our living and use our gifts, but not necessarily to devote ourselves to crazy careers which are unprofitable. In countries where Christians are persecuted, believers are passed over for promotion. They can be 'content' with menial jobs, which they would never have chosen, for the sake of Christ. Fortunately, in this country, we are not usually in that situation, though people can be passed over for promotion because they are not prepared to compromise their integrity. This should keep our focus and our perspective in balance.

If you are a single parent, you will probably need to work, but you also have to be prayerful about how you can give enough time to your children. That is the wonderful thing about being part of a Christian community. Other people are on hand to support. I remember a single parent in one of our churches who could only train as a hairdresser if people in the church were prepared to babysit for her once a week. We compiled a rota between us and managed it. Grandparents and Christian friends need to be supportive of single parents who have a hard job on their hands.

Two-parent families can also find it hard to keep going financially unless they both work. Every couple has to work out how they are going to share careers and family responsibilities. I have known men give up their jobs to stay at home with pre-school children, because it was easier for them to take a career break than it was for their wives, or because they were less fulfilled in their job. I had a friend who was a primary school teacher who decided that she could only work at executive leadership level if her husband stayed at home to look after their children while they were little. He was a social worker and decided that it was a reasonable choice for him, and everyone benefited. I have known couples who have had successful job shares. One of my sons-in-law who is a musician decided that, as most of his work was in the evening, he would be the one to do the daytime childcare while my daughter worked as a doctor. The only disadvantage was that he tended to use nap times to compose music rather than to tidy up the kitchen. In our own marriage I mainly stayed at home with our pre-school children while my husband worked full-time. But I also managed to do private tuition in the evenings to keep up my teaching skills. Later on, his unusual hours of work meant that we could share childcare, and because we lived a five-minute walk from his place of work and I had school holidays, I could work full-time. I reckoned that if he had been working in the city between 6am and 8pm as some friends did, full-time work for me would have been impossible. Individual fulfilment, a fair deal for the children – all this needs to be balanced for individual families. Otherwise, life easily descends into chaos.

Rewards for unselfishness

The African American activist Booker T Washington observed, 'The happiest people are those who do the most for others.'[16] That can sometimes involve a feeling of self-

---

[16] Booker T Washington (1856–1915) was an African American leader and educationalist, www.goodreads.com/quotes/362948-the-happiest-people-are-those-who-do-the-most-for (accessed 4th December 2024).

congratulation or self-righteousness. But many ordinary people are happy to help others. They are pleased to give to others because they can see that their gifts are useful.

If that can be true for everyone, it is particularly true for believers, because we know that God does not overlook our good works. As we noted before, we can be encouraged by the verse in Hebrews 6 'God is not unjust; he will not forget your work and the love you have shown him as you have helped his people and continue to help them.' While Matthew 6:1-4 encourages us to do good things in secret, it also says that one day God will reward us openly. There is evidence in the New Testament to show that on the Day of Judgement we will receive a reward for what we have done for Him: 'Let us not become weary in doing good, for at the proper time we will reap a harvest if we do not give up' (Galatians 6:9).

That's not the same as earning salvation, which is entirely by grace. What a relief, because if that were not true, I would always be wondering whether my good deeds were enough – and I know they are not. But God is mindful of what I have done for Him, and that might include some very patient waiting and listening. There is 'no one', says Jesus in Mark 10:29-30, 'who has left home or brothers or sisters or mother or father or children or fields for me and the gospel [who] will fail to receive a hundred times as much in this present age … and in the age to come eternal life'. And, in case you are not the 'leaving fields and going on an uncomfortable mission' sort of person, be encouraged by Jesus also saying that there is no one who has given 'a cup of water in my name' who will not receive a reward (Mark 9:41). I guess cups of tea and glasses of wine count in that too!

Using our God-given gifts brings us happiness

Will you aim at satisfaction in using your gifts for the kingdom, to make you feel content? We can't always tell what gives us satisfaction in ministry, but I have found that there are certain things which leave me with an unaccountable feeling of happiness. I use the word 'unaccountable' because they don't always count as being an important part of church service. I have organised and led children's clubs, Messy Church,[17] teaching series, the Alpha course[18] and Street Pastor patrols, because it was part of the work I was called to do and I was in part of the country where there were not too many people doing them. But I found visiting elderly people in care homes or in the community and being with patients in the wing of the local mental hospital incredibly satisfying. After I had spent an afternoon engaged in such visits, I came home with my heart singing. I would have loved to have been a church leader in a successful church with lots of Spirit-inspired modern music and outreach activities, but instead I was assigned to small struggling churches in difficult areas.

What makes your heart sing? You can't dictate or reason what that is. Nor does it necessarily chime in with any sense of success and achievement. Similarly, we might ask, which of your gifts blesses people the most? You can't dictate that either. Yes, you can plan more efficiently and develop your gifts (and it's not wrong to do so), but the effect of the gift is beyond human planning. In our present

---

[17] www.churchofengland.org/life-events/christenings/after-christening/messy-church-all (accessed 4th December 2024).
[18] www.alpha.org.uk (accessed 4th December 2024).

church, we have two administrators who work in the church office. When I phone them or consult them about a problem, I always come away feeling that they have solved everything for me, and it's a wonderful feeling. It is their gift, and they feel fulfilled by using it.

I have often been called to work at things I'm not especially gifted at – such as with small children or organising meetings – and I know enough to do them adequately. But when I use a 'real' gift, I don't consciously do anything which makes it more effective. It just is. This has to be the meaning of the word 'gift'. You are given it by God, and you haven't done anything to deserve it.

Exercising such a gift not only brings contentment but it also defies pride. I can be rightly proud because I worked hard for an exam and achieved a 'merit', but I can't be proud about something I'm not responsible for. It was a gift. When I sit next to someone in a care home and they start telling me about their problems and ask how God can help them, I don't start with an agenda. It just happens spontaneously. Similarly, if I sit in a bus and the person next to me opens up to me about their life, then it all comes from them. It is a gift from God, and I am privileged to use it.

Being greedy for other gifts

Now, me being me, I haven't always been happy about the gifts I've been given. I'd like other ones instead. I'd like to have been a brilliant academic. I'd like to have been amazingly beautiful or outstandingly good at languages. I'd like to have been a wonderful church leader or married to one, or married to a successful politician (especially if it meant being invited to lots of exciting parties). In other words, given the choice (I haven't been), I'd have loved to have been 100 per cent successful in one of these areas, without making much effort, so it's taken a lot of discipline on God's part to make me realise that that's not how I'm meant to be.

I will come to discipline later in this book because I believe that it's part of the 'slowing down' process and, without it, we will never be content with what God has assigned us to be. Romans 12:3 says, 'Do not think of yourself more highly than you ought, but rather think of yourself with sober judgment,' and Philippians 2:3 says, 'count others better than yourselves' (RSV). I'm not very good at the 'sober judgment' bit. In fact, it all sounds a bit boring. I'd prefer a bit more glamour.

But in the 'slowing down' stakes and in learning about how God wants to change us, there's no point ducking this lesson. God wants me to learn from Jesus. He didn't seem to bother about what other people thought about Him. Sometimes He was popular; sometimes He wasn't. He wasn't like a demagogue who could always rely on the mob doing what they were asked to do. He also took time to be with individuals who had no influence on anyone else. Have you ever noticed how Jesus often made the most extraordinary spiritual claims when He was with someone who didn't have the spiritual or mental capacity to understand them? Like in John 4, talking about 'true spiritual worship' with someone who had just admitted that she had had five husbands and was currently living with someone. And then when He was talking to a top intellectual leader from the Pharisees, he had the nerve to say that he needed to be 'born again' (John 3:3,7). So, if I'm going to be more like Jesus, that's the way I've got to go too – to not be bothered whether I'm talking to a person of influence or not.

Being concerned with reputation

Some gifts or professions are more highly regarded than others. I have often loved exercising the gift of teaching because it's so rewarding to help others learn some important skill, whether it's children or adults. I have found it satisfying. It's made my heart sing. But I'd far rather say, 'I'm a lecturer in English,' than, 'I'm a secondary school teacher,' because in my mind it's so much more impressive. But God showed me quite plainly in my twenties that I shouldn't pursue academia (I wouldn't have been good enough anyway, because I don't pay enough attention to detail), but that I should spend time with ordinary teenagers and see them thrive. But being a lecturer sounds so much better, and I'd like people to know I could have been one! Not much humility there, I'm afraid. The apostle John characterises love of the world as being 'the boasting of what he has and does' (1 John 2:16, NIV 1984), and says that it doesn't come from the Father. And, in fact, it will 'pass away' (v17), so it won't last and it won't bring ultimate satisfaction.

Even if I use my gifts well, I might still have to recognise that they are not as great as someone else's. In our church we have a wonderful team of preachers, and I know that many of them are more gifted than I am. But contentment shows me that God can still use me in that capacity even if I'm not the best. And even an excellent speaker in one church might not be the same as a Christian conference 'star' speaker. That might be especially hard if they think they are better at the job than the well-known speaker.

It's all to do with contentment. It might be recognising that we won't get our due thanks until we get to heaven. It might be about following the narrow path of Matthew 7:13-14. Someone might say, 'I could have been a consultant physician, but God wanted me to give my time to my disabled child.' The world, even the Christian world, may never appreciate these sacrifices, but God does. 'Humble yourselves, therefore, under God's mighty hand, that he may lift you up in due time' (1 Peter 5:6). This is not the message of 'you have to be fulfilled at all costs' or the 'look at me' fame-thirsty society we live in.

But it is the way of contentment.

Think about! *Reflections on Bible passages and your own walk with the Lord*

1. Reading the story of the slave girl who found herself in Aram in 2 Kings 5, she must have questioned why she had been placed in this situation, and maybe she never knew the consequences of the advice she had given. Review the times in your life when you have questioned why God has put you in a particular situation. Did you ever find out why?
2. Read through Isaiah 36–37. What other lessons could you learn from Hezekiah's dilemma?
3. Have you ever, like Esther, needed to pray and fast about a particular course of action? What were the consequences of your prayers and fasting?

Think about! *Your own gifts and ministry*

1. Did lockdown help you to review your ministry and gifts?
2. Have you had opportunities for ministry as a housewife or househusband, or as someone who is unemployed or retired, which have been fulfilling?
3. How has carrying out your secular job helped you to tell people about Jesus?

4
Illness and retreats

Illness is always a testing time. Visitors should be a source of comfort, but that is not the case if, as pastoral visitors, we bring glib suggestions about the cause of illness and easy advice about quick restoration to health. I often think that our motivation for giving this sort of advice is part of our tendency to want 'quick fixes' in the Christian life. In the slow lane, we come to recognise that quick fixes rarely solve problems and do not bring the relief those who we are visiting need.

Examples of illness in the Bible

The Bible shows us how people reacted to illness and sometimes why God allowed some people to suffer in this way. Sometimes He used ill-health to make people listen to Him.

Nebuchadnezzar had two bouts of feeling troubled and 'out of his mind', and each time God dealt with him in a very specific way. The first time, 'his mind was troubled and he could not sleep' (Daniel 2:1). Many of us have had similar experiences – long-term anxiety and sleeplessness. Daniel gave him the answers he was seeking, assuring him that it is God who 'reveals deep and hidden things' (v22).

While we may not be called upon to interpret people's dreams, or even, as in this case, clarify what someone's dream was, we can be sent by God to help someone who is suffering. Daniel makes it clear that he himself does not have all the answers, but 'there is a God in heaven who reveals mysteries' (v28). Like Daniel, we can be humble about our own limitations as advisors, but we can pray that God will give those who are unwell the gift of discernment about their problems. Often by asking gently probing questions, we can draw out someone's own understanding of their problems.

Listening is the key

Our biggest temptation when visiting is to say too much. A successful church leader, who was suffering from a bad bout of depression with regular panic attacks, once said that their most unwelcome visitors were those who implied they knew all the answers to the leader's problems. The leader found the attempted intervention deeply unhelpful. We should be very careful how we tread when we visit those who are ill. We shouldn't make assumptions, and we shouldn't get in God's way.

Eventually God had even more dealings with Nebuchadnezzar. The king needed to understand that he had been full of pride about his own power and majesty. He came to this conclusion of his own accord after a deeply disturbing period of illness. He was able to say, 'I … raised my eyes towards heaven, and my sanity was restored' (Daniel 4:34).

Visiting people with mental health problems

When we visit people in the mental health wing of the hospital, we need to listen more than anything else. Patients have sessions with doctors who prescribe them medications; they visit occupational therapists for art and craft sessions and physiotherapists for suitable exercises; but they have very few people to listen to their real concerns. A chaplain who is employed by a GP practice told me that she would start each session by saying, 'I have an hour; you can tell me anything you like. I am listening.' It seemed like an unimaginable luxury and her patients appreciated it. They made the most of their time each week.[19]

We may visit friends or people from church who have difficult backgrounds or diagnoses. Being able to listen to them at their own pace is a wonderful gift to give them. We don't need to share our own problems. We are simply listening to them. It is part of the 'slow down' process which we can share with others, and they will never forget this gift of time and care.

Waiting

Some people spend much of their lives waiting, but it doesn't mean that they have anyone to listen to them. The man who had been waiting at the Pool of Siloam for someone to help him into the water had been waiting for thirty-eight years (John 5:5) for the right person to come along. In all that time no one had responded to his needs.

---

[19] For more about what chaplaincy in GP work is, see The Association of Chaplaincy in General Practice, www.acgp.org.uk (accessed 4th December 2024).

No wonder he replied affirmatively to Jesus' question, 'Do you want to get well?' (v6). Some people wait for a long time for a kind friend to listen to their real desires. It is a privilege to be able to offer the service of careful and loving listening.

Even in the workplace this can be true. I had dealings with a manager of a care home who was always being told how inadequate his work was, and how to put it right. His boss emailed him constantly to tell him what to do. They never sat down face to face with him to ask him what he thought the problems were. I spent two days with him and then one whole day with his assistants, just listening as they poured out their worries. It is difficult to sort out workplace problems if no one is willing to listen. It is the gift of 'helps' which a Christian can offer.

Visiting people with chronic illness

Some people we visit have commonplace but inconvenient and sometimes very painful illnesses. It is easy to ignore someone who has had fibromyalgia, rheumatoid arthritis or Crohn's disease for a long time. Sometimes their doctors are not interested in their condition because they have heard it all before and don't have an answer. People afflicted with conditions like ME often talk about their frustration with the fact that no one really believes them when they talk about their weaknesses. I've always hated illness, not just because of the suffering, but because it stops people doing what they want to do with their lives. I know that there are no quick solutions, and I can't imagine what it feels like to be constantly slowed down by pain and exhaustion.

Hezekiah felt desperate about his illness and called out to God when he was troubled: 'Lord, come to my aid!' (Isaiah 38:14). Then he experienced God's healing and was able to confirm, 'Surely it was for my benefit that I suffered such anguish' (v17). He was also able to praise God afterwards. Later on he was healed for a defined period of fifteen years. Rather selfishly, he was thankful that he only had to worry about his lifetime and not about the difficult political relationship with Babylon which would come after his death. In Isaiah 39:8, he was relieved that 'there will be peace and security in my lifetime.'

I have a lot of sympathy with Hezekiah because I find that I can be very selfish about my own ailments and my own limited responsibilities. If I can get a quick fix from the NHS or from God, I am quite happy. I don't like to look too far ahead!

Helping those with incurable conditions

If, like me, you have very little experience of long-term physical suffering, we should be very cautious about what we say to someone in that situation. It is so easy, especially as a Christian leader, to want a quick fix for the benefit of those we visit and for our convenience. However, long-term visiting in the 'slow lane' requires a very different attitude from a cheery 'get well soon' visit, and the person will soon recognise if you are a 'please get it all together so I can tick you off my list' sort of Christian visitor.

When I was a curate, I started visiting a lady whose hip replacement had gone wrong. She couldn't walk and she was in constant pain. Her family visited her every fortnight, and carers came every lunchtime to put her food out. They came, whether it was a convenient time for her or not (a frequent problem in the official care system, when not enough time is allocated for each visit), and she was often left with congealed packet soup and unappetising sandwiches. The only useful thing I could do was to cut off the hard crusts and reheat the soup. What I learned from visiting this lady was that nothing I said could make her disability better. I might read verses of the Bible to her or pray for her, but it didn't help her situation one bit and we both knew it. My desire to 'fix things' was mainly for selfish reasons, not because of any true understanding of her circumstances.

Many months later, when I visited her in a care home and she was struggling with constant pain, she told me to go away. I felt ashamed that I had offered her so little. I wanted God to end her suffering and for me to be the person who made it all happen. I had to acknowledge in humility my own inadequacy.

Learning how to visit acceptably

I learned over the years that I had no right to think I could sort everything out for other people, and I came to accept that my companionship and prayerful love for those I visited, who were suffering, were enough. Years later at a different church I visited another lady, who was suffering with terminal cancer. I asked her if she was afraid and what she wanted me to pray for. I think by then I had learned to listen to her needs, rather than project my own on to her.

She told me that her only fear was that her husband would find caring for her physically too much for him, and she wanted her life to end before it reached that point. As I helped her husband get her ready for bed that night, I prayed about those two things. She had been given six months to live by the doctors, but that night she died in her sleep. I always felt that I had been privileged to listen to her and that God had answered our prayers.

As time went on in parish work, I felt that I had learned to care spiritually for the seriously ill because I was now no longer keen to 'prove myself' as an adequate Christian visitor. Instead, I had learned to listen and to wait on God. Being a 'helper' often means coming alongside with no expectations of solutions, just a desire to pray for and support the other person. Before I was ordained, I was always free to move on from visiting a suffering person. Being a local vicar taught me about patiently living alongside others, with no easy anticipation of the likely ending.

Visiting the sick and elderly as part of the community

One of the most skilled people I have seen working in an unobtrusive way in the community is a friend of our family. When her husband had long hours of work as part of his professional duty, this lady decided to give up her job as a nurse in order to be there for her children and to visit people in her home village in rural Germany. She told me that there were now very few people who had the time and energy to care for the elderly and sick there. She, however, did, and she never took up paid employment again. She didn't even have an official 'role' in the church, just a loving heart and a desire to draw alongside those who were ill, lonely and hurting. Great for the village that they had Suzanne living there!

Results of practising the gift of 'helps'

In the parable of the sower, it takes time for the seed to be sown and to notice obvious growth. If we go about doing the planting of the seed, which we are called to do as helpers, there will be results, even if they are not exciting, or seemingly worthy of a report in church services. One of the most wonderful things about the gift of 'helps' is that we know in our heart of hearts that it has been worthwhile, and that over time the gift has blessed others.

If God has called me to 'slow down', it is so that I can meet with people for whom time is progressing slowly. Let us never underestimate the appreciation the residents of our care homes and independent living homes have for those who come in to conduct short relevant worship services, with or without Holy Communion. There should be time afterwards when we can have an extra word with individuals who would appreciate it. I have found it so satisfying to conduct funerals for residents who I know have been reaching out to Jesus through the Eucharist and through their requests for prayer in the last months of their lives.

'Would God have time for a prodigal son?' asked one man bluntly when he came to a service. Happily, the answer is unreservedly, 'Yes!'

'Uncle Sid never went to church,' exclaimed a family who were surprised that their relative had asked me to conduct a Christian funeral service for him.

'Maybe not,' I replied, 'but over the years I saw him reach out to take Communion, and I could see how important it had become for him.' He might not have been a traditional churchgoer, but he wanted to reach out to the

Son of God, who promises, 'Whoever comes to me I will never drive away' (John 6:37).

Giving time to those who have dementia

It is easy for those who have dementia to seem the least important in our churches and in our care homes. It is obvious that the person with advanced dementia will not remember who we are, so we might ask, 'Is there any point in speaking to them?' This is when we discover that *how* we speak to someone and the feelings that we leave them with are more important than the subject of the conversation. Those of us in church leadership might remember this as a valuable lesson. Many people do not remember *what* the vicar or minister told them, but they will remember whether they felt valued.

No one with dementia in a care home will be able to report that you have been to visit, and no one will be able to recall what you discussed, but to know that someone has felt safe and happy because you have been there is a reward in itself. If, when we have visited prisoners, according to Matthew 25, we have visited Jesus, then dementia sufferers have stood in for the Lord, whenever we have been to see them. That gives a visit plenty of significance. If people with dementia have 'time shifts', then being able to relate to them by identifying with a different era or generation is worthwhile. When I visited my aunt who had advanced dementia, she was delighted that I could say that I was related to her sister (my mother) and talk to her about her schooldays as if I had enjoyed them alongside her. She also felt reassured that by being able to say the Lord's Prayer together, we could recall when she had learned it at school assembly.

Identifying with the feelings of others

Just as Jesus came to the earth and entered into our human feelings, we can enter into the feelings of people who are ill. Jesus sometimes had supernatural knowledge of illness – 'Someone touched me' (Luke 8:46), He said when He knew that power had gone out of Him to heal a woman in the crowd – but most of the time He met people on their own terms and listened to their problems. We are called to do the same.

When someone with dementia appreciates a worship service, they do so in a very special way, making it clear that they connect with what is happening. I remember a lady standing up to sing a hymn on her own and being thrilled that her memory was helping her to recall the words. If we applaud a two-year-old who chooses to recite something off by heart, why should we not affirm a dementia patient in the same way?

Holidays and retreats as time in the slow lane

If illness is a time when we can step back from our normal habits and discover a time of quiet, then that is equally true when we take a holiday or retreat.

Just recently I have been to Norfolk to stay with my sister-in-law. She lives in a beautiful house which she shared freely with us over a four-day period. We could sit on her wide, paved patio looking at her well-stocked flowerbeds first thing in the morning as we drank our coffee. We walked along the coastal path and by the side of the Broads. We had an hour's evening boat cruise in order to see kingfishers flying backwards and forwards, their feathers flashing with the light. We sat together in the quiet of the evening, looking at the reeds by the riverbank, and drank in the tranquillity without any need to talk. Human kindness and generosity made such a visit possible. We were fortunate to be the recipients of such hospitality. My sister-in-law gave us the gift of allowing us to 'slow down' in the middle of a busy life. It was different from a holiday with lots of activities and socialising. It had the effect of restoring the soul.[20]

Retreats are holidays when we more intentionally seek spiritual solace. As I do not come from a religious background where retreats were the norm, it took me some time to appreciate them. But I soon found that the joy of not having to talk to anyone, being able to sit through a meal where there was no superficial conversation, listening to beautiful music, being able to concentrate on a book, walking in nature, all had a big impact on me. Spending money on such a retreat is like deliberately putting yourself in the 'slow lane' of life and reaping the benefits.

I particularly remember participating in several retreats on Holy Island. The sense of living in the same place as the Celtic monks of old was especially inspiring. Seeing the illuminated manuscripts of the Gospels made me realise how much concentration they used, and what works of beauty were the outcome.

I have also enjoyed going to a day retreat with women from my church, when the day was also made special by a beautiful garden, a well-thought-through talk in the middle of the day and a beautifully prepared meal which demonstrated love and artistic gifts.

---

[20] Psalm 23:3.

Retreats are time in the 'slow lane' which nourish the soul and therefore our walk with the Lord. We return home better able to care for others.

Think about! *Reflections on Bible passages and your own walk with the Lord*

1. What has the experience of illness taught you personally?
2. If you have had experience of long-term illness, how does this help you to understand what other people are going through?
3. Has a holiday or retreat ever given you real relief and joy in the Christian life?

Think about! *Your own gifts and ministry*

1. If you are naturally empathetic when you visit someone who is ill, how has the Lord been able to use this gift to help others?
2. If you have visited someone on a regular basis who has long-term mental health problems, what sort of challenges have you experienced, and have you been able to resolve any of them?
3. What do you find the most difficult part of visiting people with dementia? In what ways have you found it fulfilling?

5
Gratitude and slow travel

In recent months there has been a spate of magazine and newspaper articles on the subject of gratitude. The writers have recommended various ways of practising gratitude and have informed us about how important it is for our mental wellbeing. I have no doubt about the effectiveness of such advice, and I have admiration for the entrepreneurial skills of people establishing businesses based on these principles, but I would like to raise a few questions about the basis of their beliefs.

In every area of life, gratitude is a response to a person. In no practical sense do we feel gratitude towards an impersonal object. A child feels gratitude to a family member for a special birthday treat, or an adult feels gratitude towards a friend for taking them to a hospital appointment. Whenever we receive a gift, there is always someone behind the giving.

If a convinced atheist feels glad that they don't have a cancer diagnosis, they will justifiably feel relieved or jubilant, but according to their chosen belief system, there is no one to whom they can express gratitude. If you see yourself as more of an agnostic, you might feel gratitude towards a life force (or Mother Earth, as one primary school encouraged its pupils to address the universe without using religious language), but surely you must ask yourself who is behind that force. If the good news about your health is a totally accidental piece of luck, then you might also realise that the big wheel of fortune (as the Romans saw it) could easily change its position at the next moment. This is a completely different view of gratitude from the one held by a Christian who believes in a personal God who is actively involved in His creation. Our life philosophy should inform our attitude to gratitude.

David's attitude to gratitude

Gratitude in the Bible is very closely linked with humility, and nowhere is this more apparent than in the story of David. Later in his life he wanted to bring the ark of God to Jerusalem, a city he had personally captured, but when he realised that he had not done it in the approved way, in 1 Chronicles 13:12 he asked God how it should be done. Later, as the celebrations in the city unfolded, we read in 1 Chronicles 15:27 that David the king was dressed in exactly the same way as the other Levites (the priestly caste) because he identified with them. In verse 29 he danced exuberantly before God, because he was not concerned with his own self-importance and dignity. This is also in line with his humility, when he does not consider himself good enough to marry one of the King's daughters (1 Samuel 18:18).

His gratitude and praise to God flowed naturally out of his humility. And then it spread to generosity to the people themselves, as he offered free food to them (1 Chronicles 16:3). Gratitude always has a knock-on effect in the community. It releases generosity, because the grateful person knows that they do not deserve what they have received, and therefore wants to give to others in turn, just as God has given to them.

In 1 Chronicles 17, David gets a message from Nathan the prophet, which he doesn't want to hear. He is told that he is not allowed to build the Temple himself, but instead of complaining about this disappointment, verse 16 tells us, 'King David went in and sat before the LORD.' He spends time taking in what he has been told and is grateful that God has planned a future for his family. 'You, LORD God, have looked on me as though I were the most exalted of men' (17:17). In fact, as king he *is* the most exalted of men in the country, but he knows that he is nothing compared to who God is. 'There is no one like you, LORD, and there is no God but you' (v20). He even thanks God that he and his people have the privilege of giving back to God so generously.

David's gratitude is a completely different type from that of our contemporary, secular proponents of the modern movement of 'gratitude'.

Gratitude in difficult circumstances

Gratitude is all well and good when things are going well in life, but how about when they are going badly? Do we subscribe to one of the views which was fashionable in the 1970s charismatic movement, which taught that we should thank God for everything, even the bad things? I personally don't think so because so many bad things are the result of evil and human wilfulness. However, in Philippians 4:6, Paul adds the phrase 'with thanksgiving' to his guidance about not experiencing anxiety and bringing our petitions to God. In the Bible, gratitude seems to be an attitude that should undergird all our prayers, even when we can't understand the accompanying difficult circumstances.

Paul writes in verse 12 of the same chapter that he has 'learned the secret of being content in any and every situation', and I have met older Christians who have taught me so much about that secret. They don't have the answers to all the questions about why things haven't worked out as they would have liked, but they have learned to be thankful. It's not about naivety or foolish optimism on their part. It's about trust. And trust is the key component to Christian gratitude, which sets it apart from the secular variety. People who have walked with God over a number of years, through good times and bad, have learned to praise God (like David) and be full of gratitude (like Paul). Despite their setbacks and perplexities, they are always aware of Christ's love for them. 'Thanks be to God for his indescribable gift!' (2 Corinthians 9:15) says Paul at the end of his teaching about the importance of generosity.

Beauty for ashes

Terrible and difficult events can take place in a few brief seconds, but the consequences can take a lifetime to accept. God's work does not take place in a rush. No one can easily quantify the hours of sleepless nights, self-questioning and agony endured by those who suffer. When we visit those who have been afflicted like this, we can only bow our heads in respect for the suffering endured by another human being, and trust God that the consequences somehow bring something beautiful to fruition – 'beauty for ashes' as the prophet says in Isaiah 61:3 (KJV).

My grandfather, who came from a background of grinding poverty and was illiterate before he met my grandmother as an adult, was nevertheless an enterprising and ambitious miner. The director of the mine had noticed his potential and sent him on a course of management training. While doing this, he suffered a terrible mining accident. His back was broken, and he never walked without sticks and being bent double again. He lost his livelihood and never had another day or night without excruciating pain until he died when he was seventy-two years old. My grandmother also never had an unbroken night of sleep as she nursed him. In the darkness of the mine, as he waited for help, he said to God that if he was rescued, he would give all of his life to Him. When the rescue came, he kept his side of the bargain. What he did not anticipate was the ongoing years of suffering.

Was there redemption in the suffering? Yes, in that he somehow found the resources to look after his family without any social benefits being available at the time. Yes, in that he acted as a witness and evangelist to local people and saw people become Christians. Yes, in that he passed the baton of faith down through his daughter, who became my mother and influenced my sister and me. I will never forget, as a child, seeing my grandfather, his face white with pain, bent double as he mended a toilet in order to earn money, and then return home to read his Bible. Unimaginable suffering but also unimaginable grace.

Christians believe that the slow dragging hours of suffering will be turned into the glorious 'now' of eternity, and such a belief sustains them in difficult circumstances.

Losing loved ones

I met a lady who in earlier life had lost one of her children tragically. She experienced inevitable pain and emptiness, but she also knew that months earlier the child had undergone a profound Christian conversion. And the knowledge that she would see that child in heaven took away all bitterness and gave her a reason to live. Many years later, she had the pain of seeing another of her children pass away, leaving a grieving family. She was almost overwhelmed, but she still trusted God. She recalled how God had helped her in her first tragic bereavement. She knew of no reason why she had endured these afflictions, but she knew the God in whom she needed to trust. I had the privilege of listening to her pain, and I found her attitude to be an extraordinary inspiration to me personally.

When you read the story of Horatio Spafford, who lost two of his sons to illness and then four of his daughters who drowned at sea, and realise that he wrote the hymn 'It Is Well With My Soul' after those tragedies, you know that you are treading on holy ground.[21] This was a faith forged in deep, soul-destroying experiences of the vicissitudes of life, but also knowledge that 'underneath are the everlasting arms' (Deuteronomy 33:27). When you read about the trauma of Corrie Ten Boom, as she saw her sister die in Ravensbrück concentration camp, you know that there is something greater than death and a love

---

[21] Horatio Spafford (1828–88) was an American lawyer and Presbyterian elder and Christian worker in the Middle East. For 'It Is Well With My Soul', see www.hymnal.net/en/hymn/h/341 (accessed 4th December 2024).

which overcomes all bitterness and results in amazing blessing for others.[22] Horatio Spafford and Corrie Ten Boom never lost their sense of gratitude to God.

Walking with God

These people have truly walked with God in pain, but walking with God doesn't have to mean suffering. It can mean just enjoying God's company and each other's companionship. But you can do neither if you do not slow down enough to have time to appreciate others.

Jesus managed to spend time with His Father and other human beings as He walked through first-century Palestine. There are some intriguing verses in Genesis, when we learn that 'Enoch walked faithfully with God 300 years' (Genesis 5:22). That was a lot of walking! Later, in verse 24, the text tells us that 'he was no more, because God took him away'. We can imagine that Enoch just carried on walking into the sunset and was so busy chatting to God that he didn't realise that he had continued into eternity. Sounds like a good way of going to heaven to me!

Walking with others in the countryside

Walking while chatting to God and each other is a great way of slowing down for the good of our own wellbeing and for the benefit of our relationships.

The United Kingdom is such a small island that we can access beautiful countryside from anywhere at least within a couple of hours of every city. The West Country

---

[22] Corrie Ten Boom (1892–1983) was a Dutch watchmaker, Christian speaker and writer. She tells her story in the book *The Hiding Place*.

where I live is full of old drovers' roads, many of them now sunk down below the level of modern fields. As you walk along these hidden paths, you can imagine what it was like for those driving sheep and cattle to market more than two hundred years ago.

It reminds me of the many paths and waysides described in the novels of Thomas Hardy as he traced the journey of a particular character across the countryside. When you read the detailed description of the wind and its effect on the colour of the grass and the movements of the leaves, you realise that Hardy had followed these scenes in his own experience. Even reading one of Hardy's novels slows you down as you experience the countryside through his words. They may be hard work to read and initially frustrating for today's reader, but it is a deeply rewarding experience, as one of my Year 10 classes found when they spent a term reading *The Mayor of Casterbridge* in order to complete some GCSE coursework. It's a little bit different from scrolling through social media posts, but the 'slow down' effect is worth it. Even as an older person, I have found myself hooked on my phone and have to deliberately wean myself off it while walking.

Walking with anxiety and depression

If you have a friend or family member who is suffering from anxiety or depression, then walking and not talking is a wonderful tonic, and accompanying such a person is an excellent way of offering the gift of 'helps'. We can invite someone in that situation to go out with us rather than having an intense or awkward conversation inside, when they might feel uncomfortable and embarrassed.

When you have mental health problems, seeing the wide expanses of the sky or the line of trees disappearing into the distance helps to get everything into perspective. You can become absorbed in what is going on under the surface of a pond, or you are curious as to how the stream is being damned by the beavers. My husband and I have spent whole afternoons tracking down lines of trees and high hedges which we had glimpsed from our house but which were lost to view when we drove our car. This is an alternative world to politics and the cost-of-living crisis and an uncertain future as we hear news reports about international wars. The countryside is also a real world which is worth visiting, and you emerge again into the traumatic melee of the twenty-first century feeling a little more at peace.

And while we are talking about the gift of 'helps', then walking may help our own marriage relationships. Silence is completely acceptable while walking, and, for my husband and me, we are far more at ease with each other in the country rather than being in a crowded city. We might both draw attention to different wildflowers, or buzzards hovering over us. Against the background of silence, we can hear skylarks far above. Our anxieties are soothed and calmed, and our disagreements are stilled.

Important conversations

When the right time for talking happens, it may be about important issues in the relationship, but on a walk there is less likelihood of becoming combative. Walking also offers opportunities to explore deep philosophical questions.

The Coleridge Way over the Quantock Hills, on the edge of Exmoor, reminds us that two famous poets,

Wordsworth and Coleridge, who were also friends, sorted out their philosophy while taking this route (before they moved to the Lake District). They thrashed through the meaning of the French Revolution, which was taking place on the other side of the Channel, as they walked and talked. Friends or spouses may move through deeply held theological differences as well but, somehow, as they stop to watch the heron rise on the opposite riverbank to protect their young from human intruders, they are not so inclined to feel prickly and upset about different and controversial points of view.

Encountering strangers in a relaxed way

As you move along the path, you encounter strangers, and it gives you a new perspective on life. I have a friend who generally feels too shy to talk in social situations, but if you find yourself on a walk with him, he always has the right observation or joke for the person he encounters along the way. He is at ease, and it boosts his confidence.

Everyone seems to want to have a word with you as you pass by. 'Oh, did you know that this is the Two Moors Way and not the Macmillan Way West?' they observe as though it's an important point to make.

'Oh, really? We didn't realise they converge here. Glad to have met you!'

'How lovely to see someone consulting a paper map rather than a phone app,' approves an older female villager.

'Where do you come from?' and the conversation is off to a flying start.

We can be encouraged by the generosity of local people. On entering a pub, my husband and I realised that we had ordered our drinks before noticing that they would not accept a bank card as payment. 'Never mind,' said the landlady of the pub on the Somerset Levels. 'Come and join us anyway,' she added, pushing two dogs away and telling us all about their state of health. 'It doesn't matter about the payment.'

During the Covid pandemic, we walked through a Somerset village where Christmas scenes had been created in the front windows of houses and in specially constructed grottos by the wayside. 'We can't talk together or go into a church,' a resident explained from a few yards away, 'but we do need to remind each other about what happens at this time of year, so this way we can look at each other's Christmas memories, whether we are religious or not.' How right they were! Sharing art can be more powerful than words, which is why creating craft in a care home can be so rewarding as part of the service.

'I've still got the Easter box you helped us make,' a member of staff told me after I had helped at an activity event. 'I keep it on my mantelpiece to remind me what it's all about.'

Getting out of our cars

I think God specially created tractors in the West Country to disrupt everyone's car journeys and force drivers to talk to each other! Sometimes the tractors are old and mud-spattered, and they can hold you up for miles on the country lanes; sometimes they are new, sophisticated monsters worth thousands of pounds. I have been part of a queue of cars which were forced to the side of a long winding hill as a massive vehicle with three new tractors on its back tried to negotiate a sharp corner. Everyone was out on the road, sharing advice about how the tractors were going to arrive at their destination of the local farm and how we were going to avoid being squashed.

I have been marooned in the middle of a traffic jam on the M5 with everyone out on the tarmac sharing bottles of water in the heat, and found myself giving impromptu advice to a couple who couldn't decide whether to stay in London or return to the West Country after their retirement. I have been stuck on a narrow, cliff-side road because all traffic had been diverted there away from the main road through Devon because of an accident. It was one track only with a few passing places, and when a 4x4 broke down and the rescue vehicle couldn't get through, we all gave up on our schedules for the evening and decamped to the farmer's yard to park our cars and exchange life stories. Circumstances of life force us to slow down, and we are all the better for it.

Inspired by older pilgrims

We often walk the land following God's servants from centuries ago, whose lives were touched by Him. We were walking in Wales (only a couple of hours from home) when we came across a small church which had been built by a Celtic warrior in the eighth century, when he had lost his way and asked God to help him. It was in the middle of the countryside, and we experienced the extraordinary peace of God as we sat within the entrance gate and ate our picnic. We felt the continuity of Christian witness as we realised that the church was still being used by the modern-day Welsh Anglican Church. They kept it open all day for people to come and pray there, providing free tea, coffee and cold drinks to refresh visitors. As they left the church open and did not personally serve the refreshments, church members were pleased to serve those they would never meet.

Hospitality takes time and derives from a generous spirit. It was exactly that same spirit which prompted the Corinthian and Macedonian churches to give either out of their poverty or out of their more plentiful resources, as Paul explains in the second letter to the Corinthians.[23]

Generosity received and given

Receiving the gift of the beauty of God's creation inspires us to give to others not only in material goods but also in time. To slow down in walking is to become open to others to understand what is really happening in their lives. It was when the car I was using for parish work broke down and when we could not afford an immediate replacement that I learned the joy of daily walking up and down my parish in Salford. My schedule was slowed down but my encounters with people on the street and in the shops were multiplied, and therefore the opportunities for ministry enlarged. Generosity rooted in gratitude is sharing who we are in the 'slow lane' of life and therefore really understanding what the gift of 'helps' entails.

---

[23] 2 Corinthians 8:2.

Think about! *Reflections on the Bible passages and your own walk with the Lord*

1. What examples from David's prayer of thanksgiving in 1 Chronicles 16:8-36 might inspire you personally?
2. In 1 Chronicles 29:14, David seems to see giving back to God as being an enormous privilege. What can we learn about our own attitude to giving from David's words?
3. In what circumstances of life have you learned the secret of 'being content in … every situation', as Paul talks about in Philippians 4:12?

Think about! *Your own gifts and ministry*

1. Have you ever had to hand over to someone else in a ministry which you had anticipated completing? How did that make you feel?
2. Have you ever found it difficult to know what to say when visiting someone who has experienced great suffering in their lives? How did you navigate that problem? Looking back at the incident, would you change anything of what you said?
3. Have you ever been inspired by someone else's testimony of God's sustaining power in great hardship? How did this act as a role model for you as you considered hardship?

6
Kindness

God's foundational quality passed down to us

I feel comforted that the Bible speaks about God's compassion and unfailing love, and also about His kindness. In Psalm 119, the psalmist hopes that this quality of God's character may reassure him: 'Let ... thy merciful kindness be for my comfort' (Psalm 119:76, KJV). In Luke 6:35, Jesus teaches us that 'the Most High ... is kind to the ungrateful and wicked'. As a consequence of this foundational attribute of God, Paul exhorts us in Ephesians 4:32, 'Be kind and compassionate to one another, forgiving each other, just as in Christ God forgave you.'

Kindness is demonstrated in some of the small 'vignettes' in several Bible stories. Think of the character of Dorcas (or Tabitha) who 'was always doing good and helping the poor' (Acts 9:36). We read about her in the context of Peter's gift of healing, as she was raised from the dead, but her gift of 'helps' had already been much appreciated by the local church, because in those times the widows would have had no outside financial support and so the gifts of clothing from Dorcas were very welcome (v39).

Barnabas (whose name means 'son of encouragement', Acts 4:36) went to the trouble of introducing the newly converted Paul to the church in Jerusalem, when they were unsure about whether he was a genuine Christian (Acts 9:27). Barnabas believed in Paul and was his partner in his early missionary adventures, and later he chose to encourage John Mark who had previously let Paul down (Acts 15:37-39). Barnabas was someone who believed in giving young Christians a second chance. In his life we see that kindness often led to encouragement of others – all part of the gift of 'helps'. Time is of the essence if we are to practise kindness

Kindness in the pandemic

'Kindness,' said Goethe, 'is the golden thread that holds society together.'[24] We certainly witnessed that during the Covid lockdowns, when we saw people checking up on others, taking shopping to isolated people each week, going to the pharmacy for their prescriptions, establishing WhatsApp community groups and offering to phone and listen to people who were lonely. As well as demonstrating a sense of duty, there were genuine acts of kindness, and it made people feel good about themselves. It was partly because most people had more time to do other things – the phone calls, the quizzes on Zoom, the community singsong online. Many weren't rushing to go out to work. We had time, and those of us who had family at home found ways of enjoying ourselves. The daily hour

---

[24] Johann Wolfgang von Goethe (1749–1832) was a German philosopher and writer, www.azquotes.com/quote/946115 (accessed 12th December 2024).

allowed for exercise seemed like an exciting focus for the day. We sat out on our decking, enjoying our morning coffee and snack lunches. When we turned on the news at six o'clock, it felt like we were gathering with the whole country to find out who had suffered and who had helped others. We were so glad to take an old laptop to a charity who were repurposing computers for schoolchildren who couldn't work online at home. How we wanted to help the children who were disadvantaged!

I think about the case reported from Italy during the early days of the pandemic. The hospitals were in chaos, unable to cope with the numbers of seriously ill people who were being admitted. The young doctors were overworked and unable to cope. Into a ward walked a pastor in his seventies. He had no PPE, but he chose to sit alongside the dying, to hold their hands, to tell them about God's love and to pray for the medical staff. The doctors there, who described themselves as atheists, reported that immediately the pastor came, the atmosphere on the ward changed. An extraordinary sense of hope and peace was born. Of course, the pastor eventually succumbed to the virus himself, but the doctors reported that everything had changed, and they experienced this supernatural peace. Never again would they dismiss belief in God as being pointless.[25]

The pastor's action was kindness taken to the extreme, and he did it because of his living hope in the resurrection.

---

[25] Reported incident in Lombardy in *InTerris* online international magazine by Manuela Petriri, 21st March 2020. Similar incidents also took place through the unselfishness of Catholic priests. See *The New York Times* article by Jason Horowitz and Elisabetta Povoledo, 11th April 2020.

It was self-sacrifice, but nevertheless a form of kindness; and it demonstrates why I appreciate kindness so much. It means someone stopping and going out of their way to consider the needs of someone else when they don't need to do so.

Small kindnesses are an extra in life

A small kindness happens every day when someone allows you to come out of a side road onto a busy main road when there are no natural spaces in the traffic. I always feel that sort of action sets you up for the day – both offering and receiving it. In evolutionary terms it is unnecessary. It achieves nothing for the person who is offering the kindness, but everything for the person who receives it.

It means so much to receive a gift which is given unnecessarily for the sheer joy of generosity. It requires the giver and the receiver to slow down. It is a moment of beauty, when someone else's heart reaches out to you. The giver immediately perceives that the recipient needs help, and wants to give it. It feels extraordinary. It feels as though there is hope for all humankind because of it – especially when it comes from a stranger.

I suppose that is why the story of the good Samaritan in Luke 10 speaks to us so powerfully. We often focus on the fact that it was an unacceptable foreigner who looked after the man, and of course that is true. But what happens if we just focus on the sheer kindness of the action and what it meant to the person receiving it, irrespective of the giver's cultural origin? The act of kindness is an exuberant extra in life – totally unnecessary, but when you look back on it, you wonder how you could have managed without it. It gave you hope; if you were going through a down time, it seemed to set your trajectory on the upward path, so that suddenly anything seemed possible.

We have observed the response to kindness on our television news programmes when we have seen people offer rooms in their homes to those escaping from war in Ukraine. The recipients of this hospitality spoke of how this offer changed their lives, not just by being given a roof over their heads, but by being given a new start in education or finding a job, or finding a new future for their children.

I observed the same reaction when I saw a charity's film about pastors in Ukraine going with food parcels into the war zones, finding people left behind on the front line and connecting with them. The recipients of the kindness didn't just say, 'Thank you for the food. It saved me from hunger.' They said, 'Thank you that we have been remembered. Thank you that you see me as important.' Older people in a village on the front line might well feel insignificant because of their age, because of their incapacity, because of their lack of economic and social status. But the gifts changed their perception of themselves. They started to feel hopeful.

My own changing attitude to kindness

I am ashamed to say that earlier in my life, I didn't think very highly of kindness. It didn't fit in with my ambition, my desire to achieve. It seemed too little, too soft and too weak. It didn't make a strong statement. It took up too much time which I felt could have been spent on something more focused. Such a warped understanding led to some wrong attitudes in my Christian life which

God needed to change. But now I can admit that kindness has been something which has touched me more than anything else in life. When I've been depressed, kindness has lifted my spirits. When I've felt that the world is a cold, hard place, kindness from others has given me permission to be a little bit softer on myself. Other people's kindness makes me feel that I am a worthwhile person. I may have been brought up in a good home, but the extra kindness from people outside the family has had an extraordinarily beneficial effect. I am so grateful to those who have been kind to me.

Kindness is done for no other reason than it is an instinctive feeling on the part of the person who is giving it. It doesn't always obviously achieve anything. It is not done for an ulterior motive. There is no thought of a payback. It is about thinking about what would brighten up someone's day. It might even be considered a complete waste of time in terms of achievement. I think it makes you aware of love like nothing else. It is entirely gratuitous. It makes someone stop and draw into a lay-by or do an unnecessary detour, and it somehow makes life more meaningful. Without a softening of the heart, kindness cannot function.

Kindness as part of the gift of 'helps'

Christians discuss what they think the greatest gift is, but I think they often overlook kindness. It's not mentioned as a spiritual gift as such, but it makes so much difference to someone's life, which is why I would include it as part of the gift of 'helps'. How you do something in church is influenced by kindness. You can offer someone a cup of tea after church in a matter-of-fact way, or you can do it with kindness.

I once had a member of my congregation who complained that she didn't like modern Christian music because it wasn't what her mother had known. The conversation wasn't getting very far, but then I remembered the way she served tea. She always enquired kindly about the person's week. She noticed whether the colour they wore suited them. She always had a little extra word to say which made that person feel special.

'When you come to church,' I assured her, 'you might not like the music, but you are contributing to the way we are at church. You give so much love to the people who come in, and that is an important way of doing church. Thank you.'

I never heard her complain about modern music again.

Kindness in marriage

I have found that I don't easily forget someone else's kindness. I go back to it again and again in my mind. It makes me feel special and worthwhile. It has the effect of making me want to be kind too. My mother used to say that when you are looking for a husband, kindness is the most important quality of all. Why is that? Because the husband often has the position of power and strength, so unkindness can be a very frightening quality in someone in that position.

When my mother spoke, I was very dismissive of the idea. I thought it sounded weak and unexciting. I thought it was more important to have a husband who achieved things and took risks. Now, looking at all the failed marriages I've witnessed, I know that my mother was right and that kindness should be given top priority. Why are we so unkind to our nearest and dearest when we would never have that attitude to a friend or even a stranger?

Sadly, I have come across many married people who have felt that their spouse's criticisms have been totally justified, including one who had been given a long list of all the mistakes they had made, and why those mistakes were particularly annoying and unacceptable. I couldn't help thinking how my husband could have made a similar list and added in many worse traits that I displayed in my character. Kindness excuses the bad qualities and sees the good qualities instead. 'Love bears all things, believes all things, hopes all things' (1 Corinthians 13:7, RSV). You might be unaware of someone's faults when you marry them, but after a few years you will know them well. And they will have the capacity to irritate you. It is only kindness, grounded in love, that will keep you from concentrating on them and also allow you and your partner to accept and love each other.

Kindness as the bedrock of our church life

When our children were little, life was hard and no one in the church had much extra time to give to me. I went to a Bible study where the leader asked which was the most important spiritual quality for each of us to desire. In a very small voice, I said, 'The gift of kindness.' It sounded a lot less spiritual than anyone else's choice, but I felt it deeply. I was desperate for kindness. I felt I was surrounded by people who were hard, and who didn't appear to have time to be kind. Maybe they weren't receiving much kindness themselves! They knew all the right answers from the Bible, but I felt the lack of love in the group. I felt that the Christian life was just one hard slog. A little superfluous kindness would have made all the difference.

I have talked to two young mums recently who both said how hard it was when their children misbehaved in church. They felt that people looked at them with judgement or with pity. They just wanted another adult to be interested in them and to ask them how they were doing. In that situation I always make it my business to tell parents the worst stories of my children's misbehaviour in church (I have quite a few to share!).

It can be particularly hard when a child has special educational needs, such as attention-deficit/hyperactivity disorder (ADHD) or autism spectrum disorder (ASD). It is so important for older Christians to get alongside the parent and help them to feel that they are doing a good enough job in difficult circumstances, and perhaps ask them what they would most value – going with them as a family to a park, babysitting, going for a coffee with you.

I remember when a family in our church invited us out for tea on Boxing Day. I had spent all Christmas trying to make everything nice for my family, and since I had no extended family in the area to support me, I felt exhausted. That invitation to tea lifted my spirits and made me excited about the day ahead. I felt as though I had been given something special.

Prayer as kindness

When someone makes a special point of praying for you, it also feels like a kindness. Recently, two members of our adult family and one grandchild have been seriously ill.

After I put their names on the church prayer chain request list, several people came up to me and asked me how they were doing. They mentioned their names and showed that they knew all the details of the problems. It wasn't just the first week when it came in as news. It was several weeks later when the situations were no longer 'newsworthy'. Those people were clearly praying for my family, and I appreciated it. Every time someone mentioned their names, I felt warmed by their kindness, even when I didn't know the person who was praying well. If you believe in a God who answers prayer, then the greatest kindness you can offer is to pray for someone with sensitivity and intelligence.

Small kindnesses as ministry and as part of chaplaincy

It's easier to be kind when you have a little bit more money and time, and I like to think that now that I do have those commodities, I can give some gratuitous kindness – a small message of appreciation in a notelet, a telephone call because you notice that someone has been away (though if you do this, you need to be careful that you are not checking up on their church attendance!), a plant bought to cheer someone up, an extra meal made. If I have a ministry in retirement, it's the gift of 'helps'– time to do a bit of extra babysitting, or to take some kids out to the park for an overburdened mum, or to spend time chatting to someone who is lonely. I want to point people to Jesus, because He must be the most important person of all, but whether the person is a believer or not, it feels like a small service to show kindness.

I think that my job as an Anna Chaplain can be summed up in the word 'kindness'. How can I make someone feel better? How can I cheer them up? How can I get them to laugh? How can I help meet their needs when they are sad? How can I listen to them when they have no one else who will?

I love the look on our residents' faces when I am able to give them a prize for bingo or winning a game. Two years ago, I felt happy when, through a gift made by a charity, I was able to buy a book about Queen Elizabeth's life and faith and give it to them; and when I was able to give one to a member of staff, who was a recent immigrant, she was really touched by it. Some older residents and staff receive very little from anyone. They have to pay for everything, even the attention of their family. I knew an elderly person who lived very near her teenage grandchildren, but when she needed help from them with the shopping, she had to give them money in return. How about getting something for nothing? Isn't that what grace is all about?

Kindness within families

I remember my mother's delight in her later years when she received a small posy on Mothering Sunday at a church. My mother had given so much to so many people, especially in cooking meals, and it meant a lot to her to receive something freely. I realise to my shame that I had always been receiving things from her and I gave very little back.

When recently the way has been hard in coping with illness in our family, my daughter who lives locally has made a point of inviting us, her parents, for a meal, making the atmosphere nice and getting just the right level of conversation. I have felt so uplifted by those evenings. I know that it takes a lot of energy to do that when you have three very small children at home with you all the time, and her sacrifice has meant a lot to me.

Kindness comes from not judging

I'd like to be kind not only in what I do, but also in my attitude to people. That means crediting them with the best motives and seeing that if they are difficult, it's often because they've been hurt in some way themselves. When people are offhand and unreliable, it's often because something else is going on in their lives. When I found myself being critical of someone not turning up to be part of a church team, I later found out that they had just had a difficult experience at work. I found one of our new young people to be really argumentative, and then learned that they had suffered a bereavement the year before. I remember that when I taught adolescents, we would often discover that a youngster who was difficult and rude in class had been experiencing a parental break-up. Among teenagers in school I encountered a lot of buried hurts, which were freely shared with an adult when they were the recipients of kindness. And this is true of adults too. That doesn't excuse all bad behaviour, but it does mean, as well as order and control, it is worthwhile trying to find out more about what is going on in a person's life.

Kindness making a world of difference

When you are supporting someone with mental health challenges, kindness means so much. When you are caring for someone close to you, you don't want to be disloyal. You don't want to complain about how hard it is, so you need someone else to enter imaginatively into your world.

You need someone to understand, to see that you might be putting on a good show, but underneath you are hurting.

When someone in your family has mental health difficulties, such as serious depression, you don't want to complain about it. You don't want to explain that this brings you down too, that someone else continually seeing the bad side of things can make you feel sad. When someone close to you is always seeing the bad side of things and never wants to have fun, it can make you feel miserable. In those circumstances, someone's kindness can make all the difference in the world. It can lift you up. If they give you a compliment, it can make you feel that you are not failing after all – that you are doing your best in very difficult circumstances, and you feel affirmed. You know that at least one person sees beneath the surface – sees that you are putting up with criticism or bad temper and appreciates that you are doing your best to remain pleasant and positive and rational.

It is often easier to see what someone is suffering when they are looking after someone who is physically disabled. The extent of the carer's work and unselfishness is apparent. It is less so when they are caring for someone who is forgetful, bad-tempered and critical. When someone feels no hope for the future, it brings their companion down too. A kind thought from someone outside the situation makes all the difference. However good a counsellor or psychiatrist is (and that level of professional support may be very important), the joy of knowing someone who shows empathy and who is not being paid for what they do is amazing. Knowing that someone understands and appreciates what you are doing makes all the difference.

Some people are given very few kindnesses in their lives. I remember a lady I knew who had been 'married off' as a young woman to an alcoholic, to relieve the parents' financial burdens, when she had only just escaped her father's alcoholism. Later in life she had found some relief in a happy second marriage, when suddenly her husband died. After that she was always rescuing her adult children when they had made bad choices, earning a basic living because she didn't have the qualifications to do anything else, and finally babysitting and feeding grandchildren who didn't have anyone else to care for them. Not a lot of opportunity to receive kindness there – only give, give, give from her meagre resources.

Kindness opens up the heart to God

It is, of course, only God who can meet the needs of the heart that is hurting, but folk are opened up to the love of God by the kindness of another human being who has time for them. Apparently, after a recent devastating earthquake in a country not sympathetic to the gospel, it has been small groups of Christians who have reached some of the most out-of-the-way places and have been able to offer food and shelter to the victims. 'Why are you doing this for us when no one else is interested?' they have asked their rescuers. The love of God in Christian action speaks for itself.

We cannot have time for everyone. But that doesn't mean that we can't do anything. We can. Jesus said that even a cup of water given in His name would not be forgotten.[26] That must mean that basic kindness is very

---

[26] Mark 9:41.

important to God. In his last sermon before his death, St David, the patron saint of Wales, told his congregation that not only should they rejoice in God, but they should also be content to do small things for Him. A little note of thanks and appreciation put through the door can mean so much to someone.

As Christians, we too can face difficult circumstances. We are not exempt from the trials of life – unexpected losses, financial difficulties, family problems – but through them we can prove God's love and enjoy other Christians who reach out to us. And somehow that makes the trial more bearable.

A heartfelt 'thank you' can make all the difference. Earlier in life, when I had worked hard at organising the youth group weekend, doing the cooking and cleaning and booking, no one bothered to say 'thank you' apart from the mother of one child who had just joined the group. She texted me to say how much her child had enjoyed the weekend and she wanted to say 'thank you'. It made all the hard work worthwhile.

Servant-hearted Christianity

My husband is above all kind, and it comes over to the people who meet him. He will often exhaust himself looking after young children, but they all love being with him. When we helped to lead a children's camp in North Africa one summer, after the sessions had finished he always had two or three little children who trailed after him for the rest of the day. They could hardly communicate in their own language, but they recognised his love. He will often take over practical jobs, like making tea for everyone at church after the service. It might not be up there in the list of top spiritual gifts, but it is the gift of 'helps' and everyone benefits from it.

I appreciate the people in church who are servant-hearted, not those who find fault, not the people who want to show you they know all the denominational rules, not those who want everything done perfectly; rather, those who volunteer for an extra shift on Street Pastors, those who bake a cake for our youth weekend, those who take the time to say that they appreciate an activity or a sermon.

Kindness demonstrating the love of Jesus

Kindness is putting yourself in a position of weakness, because through it, you don't get to be top dog. Jesus was kind – blessing the children, who the disciples found to be a nuisance; turning round to find the person who had touched Him in the crowd. And Jesus was also the strongest person of them all. Kindness means that you don't always have your own way; you don't get to tell the funniest story or have everyone pay attention to you. You miss out on the glory.

Kindness adds some beauty to life, just because making life beautiful for someone else can be such a beautiful thing to do.

I'd like to have more time to show kindness, not to become impatient with someone who doesn't understand something quickly – a child, or an adult who has learning difficulties or is suffering from dementia. How wonderful just to take time to be with someone and to let them know that they are valued and accepted. It's a danger in care homes that staff won't have time for that. They're too busy delivering medication or arranging activities, when the resident really needs time. I am blessed in my role as chaplain because I quite often have time to listen to someone when no one else does. Last week I sat with someone in his nineties who is profoundly deaf but is very intelligent and has ideas he wants to communicate. Normally no one has time to repeat things slowly and carefully, to turn towards him so that he can lipread easily, but also to say things that show understanding of the subject matter he thinks about deeply. But I did have that time, and I was privileged to use it so well.

Think about! *Reflections on Bible passages and your own walk with the Lord*

1. In what ways have you experienced 'the kindnesses of the LORD'?[27]
2. Have you ever been touched by an unexpected piece of kindness from someone in your church?
3. In Ephesians 4:32, we are told to show our kindness in the way we forgive 'each other, just as in Christ God forgave you'. Reflect on a time when you needed to show kindness as you deliberately forgave someone else. Did this cost you a lot personally, and have you had to repeat the process of forgiveness on several occasions? What happened when you did?

Think about! *Your own gifts and ministry*

1. Have you ever acted as a Barnabas in your ministry? Was it fulfilling, and why?
2. Did you find yourself carrying out a role of kindness either during the pandemic or during the cost-of-living crisis, either in your church or in your neighbourhood?
3. What is your experience of dealing with people who have mental health difficulties in your church?

---

[27] Isaiah 63:7.

7
Purpose and prayer

Older years, and outwardly physically or mentally inactive years (through being a carer or having childcare responsibilities), can be very challenging. These are times when the evil one can attack us, and we need all the spiritual armour at our disposal in order to fight him. 1 Peter 5:8 tells us that 'the devil prowls around like a roaring lion looking for someone to devour'. If we're not careful, we can be the ones who get devoured. As we go through time in the 'slow lane', we need to have a purpose so we know that what we are doing is worthwhile.

The armour of God

That's when the armour of God, described in Ephesians 6:10-19, comes in handy. In verse 12 we are reminded that 'our struggle is not against flesh and blood, but against the rulers, against the authorities, against the powers of this dark world and against the spiritual forces of evil in the heavenly realms'.

That means that even if we are physically inactive, we don't have to be spiritually inactive. We can still have 'feet fitted with the readiness that comes from the gospel of peace' (v15). There may still be lots of opportunities to meet with people and to share the gospel. When I was part of a secular mums and toddlers' group, I had lots of opportunities to share the good news, and as a result of all my contacts and friendships there, I was able to start a small seekers' group in my house, even though children were always interrupting. A friend, who is more or less confined to her house through looking after her husband, sometimes picks up her grandchildren from the school round the corner. Through her conversations in the playground, she has had the opportunity to meet young mothers in distress and to reassure them and pray for them.

Verse 16 talks about taking up 'the shield of faith' and being able to 'extinguish all the flaming arrows of the evil one'. In the next verse it mentions 'the sword of the Spirit, which is the word of God'. In our various situations in the 'slow lane' of life, there will be lots of room for doubt and fear. Why are we here? How long is this trial going to go on for, and will I last the course? How can I cope with being so bored? How does this all fit in with the purpose of my life? Does God know about this, or even care? These are all questions I have asked myself through the times of trial in my own life.

The 'shield of faith' can often be used through reading or quoting Scripture to ourselves or singing a well-remembered chorus or hymn. You don't need long, drawn-out Bible sessions to do this. A daily verse from a Bible app on your phone can be just what you need, even if you need someone from the younger generation to set it up in the first place. When I was visiting an experienced Christian who had been disabled mentally and physically through a stroke, he told me that one of the most helpful aids he had been given was a Lifewords booklet, *Daily*

Strength.[28] The format of a verse or two a day for a month has helped many people I visit. I now always carry one round with me for giving away.

Having an aim for our older years?

If 'older years' means only having a cup of tea at the local garden centre and, if you are rich enough, going on a cruise, then you are likely to be lacking in purpose. That not only feels sad but it is also not what New Testament Christianity is all about. You don't find Paul looking back at a life lacking in purpose. This is the man who wrote at the end of his life, 'I have fought the good fight.' Nor was he lacking a goal for the future: 'Now there is in store for me the crown of righteousness' (2 Timothy 4:7-8). So, with failing health and fewer choices, what can we find to do in the 'slow lane' of life? It is true that we might need to manage our expectations, but we can still have them.

The role of grandparents

Grandchildren (and no doubt great-grandchildren) are a joy, and though as Christians we don't want to be exclusively preoccupied with our families, there are moments to be treasured. 'Look, Nanna,' says two-year-old Sam as he climbs up the chainmail rope by himself for the first time and arrives at the top with a huge sense of achievement. 'Look at my ballet dress,' glows Debbie delightedly, twirling her skirt for me on a visit to London. One of the pleasures of being in the 'slow lane' is that you

---

[28] Produced by Lifewords global charity, www.lifewords.global (accessed 5th December 2024).

don't have to find or wash all their kit, and instead you can just be there to admire.

At the heart of the extended family

As Christians, we may have a deeper role than just being an ornamental extra for our families. I know someone who supports her daughter who has an over-busy domestic situation and a full-time job, and she gets up early every morning to travel to the other side of the city to look after several children before they go to nursery and school. That takes some self-sacrifice but is so valuable.

Listening to our grandchildren may have a wonderful psychological and spiritual benefit. I have known several grandparents who are the prayer warriors of their extended family, not just because of their spiritual maturity, but also because they have the time available. We can have family WhatsApp groups which are centres for prayer requests as well as celebrations of photos and videos. When you have family all round the world, this is particularly useful. How wonderful to be able to use technology to send a quick SOS to the older generation for prayer support.

One of my best friends lives in Worcestershire in a 'granny flat' attached to her son's house, and her other children live quite nearby. Whenever I call on her, I find teenage grandchildren stopping to have a chat after school. Technically they are checking up on her, but they are also sharing their needs with her after their school or college day, because they know she listens, offers good advice and prays for them. Her husband had a similar role and, after he passed away, his grandchildren felt the loss keenly.

Active lives for God in retirement

More active older people are busy practising their gifts in a wider field. At our church, Ruth has been organising the mums and toddlers' group for thirty years. She knows generations of local children and she prays for them. At eighty-six years of age, she is now considering passing on the responsibility to someone younger! Recently she met an older man in the churchyard who was enduring a pressing problem. They sat and talked together on the bench. 'How come you're always there at the right time?' he asked her. It could be the guidance of the Holy Spirit, and her gifts of wisdom, discernment and 'helps'.

My sister and her husband spent a very active retirement involved in a medical missionary association working in Eastern Europe and Africa,[29] and my sister also worked with a mission among Jewish people. They didn't just work in an administrative role; they were out there, supporting churches and charities in Eastern Europe and involved in teaching English as a foreign language – something they would not have had the time for when they were both working full-time.

Our church has a team of Christians Against Poverty volunteers, and the leader uses her retirement to organise this very worthwhile charity in our area to help those who need extra food and debt advice.[30] Many older people from our church contribute the gift of 'helps' by giving a constant supply of extra tinned goods and praying.

---

[29] www.mmn.uk.com (accessed 16th December 2024).
[30] Christians Against Poverty was started in 1996 by John Kirby. www.capuk.org (accessed 5th December 2024).

Tony, whose wife had dementia for twenty years, has spent his 'spare' time both while she was ill and after she died in founding and running the Bristol Dementia Action Alliance, which has been a blessing to so many.[31] He hasn't spent his time sitting around feeling sorry for himself.

Older people don't have to give up

In one of my former churches, a lady in her nineties was always looking for ways of telling other people about Jesus. As she couldn't work with children any more, she prayed for them and was always asking me what I was doing for them. She had always been a staunch supporter of the Gideons,[32] and when she had to go to hospital because of a broken hip, one of the first things she noted was that hers was the only bedside locker without a Gideons' New Testament in it. She continued drawing attention to this omission until the hospital staff addressed it. I have never known anyone recover from a broken hip so quickly. She saw her fall as a circumstance which, although a trial, was allowed by the Lord to help others spiritually. Later, when she had to spend a few months in a care home, she made sure that copies of the church magazine were on display in the social area and passed them around. She was on a mission right to the end of her life.

---

[31] Bristol Dementia Action Alliance, www.bdaa.org.uk (accessed 5th December 2024). Also see Tony's book about his experience: Tony Hall, *A Bucketful of Patience*, Bristol: Bristol Books CIC, 2023.
[32] The Gideons International, founded in 1899 in Janesville, Wisconsin, seek to distribute Bibles throughout the world, www.gideons.org (accessed 7th February 2025).

My brother-in-law, a retired consultant psychiatrist, spends some of his retirement helping inform people about mental health issues using a book he wrote some years ago, relating his Christian faith to the associated problems.[33]

Disappointment or fulfilment?

I regularly meet old people who are disappointed with life and have become sad or bitter. I also meet Christians who have suffered disappointment but have turned from that emotion to find fulfilment in the Lord. They are not naïve about problems in their lives, but they have not allowed bitterness to dominate them. I always find them an inspiration. They are looking for 'a better country – a heavenly one' (Hebrews 11:16), and they make their focus very clear. While they may enjoy material or family benefits, they are 'looking forward to a new heaven and a new earth' (2 Peter 3:13). Are they anticipating disappointment? Not at all! Because they know that, unlike the old world, the new one will be 'where righteousness dwells'. Living in a small house or flat or even one room is not a problem for them, because their eyes are not set on earthly possessions.

By contrast, I once met a man who suddenly realised that his world-travelling job and huge house had not been enough to bring him real joy, especially when his marriage broke up. Suddenly he thought about God for the first time in forty years, when he attended a service in his care home.

---

[33] Dr Stephen Critchlow, *Mindful of the Light*, Watford: Instant Apostle, 2016.

A former RAF pilot who was a committed Christian found himself in a care home, without family and suffering from increased confusion and memory problems. He often could not find his way back to his own room on the corridor. He looked at similarly placed people around him and said to me, 'I don't know how they manage without God.' His life of faith has shown him that he has a rock to rely on, and others – staff and residents – noticed his resilience and positive attitude.

Bible characters and prayer

Paul never had a problem about what to do with his time. Even when he was in prison he prayed, so in Ephesians 6:18 he gives this injunction, 'And pray in the Spirit on all occasions with all kinds of prayer and requests. With this in mind, be alert and always keep on praying for all the saints' (NIV 1984). Prison didn't prevent him from preaching the gospel either. In verses 19 and 20 he writes, 'Pray also for me, that whenever I open my mouth, words may be given me so that I will fearlessly make known the mystery of the gospel, for which I am an ambassador in chains. Pray that I may declare it fearlessly, as I should' (NIV 1984). I'm not sure that Paul needed to ask that he might declare the gospel fearlessly, because he seemed to do that all the time, but he asked anyway!

Prayer affects our witness

If we're incapacitated in one way or another (such as being ill, or housebound, or simply just having no transport), can we still pray for the salvation and wellbeing of others? My experience is that the answer is a resounding 'yes'!

I visited a sheltered housing home on a regular basis at one point in my ministry as a chaplain, and there I met a lady in her nineties, called Janice. When Janice went to live there, the rules of the house forbade residents to proselytise. As this was obviously the right home for her for other reasons, she rather reluctantly signed the agreement and took it to the Lord in prayer. When I met her, she said to me, 'I was upset because I thought I couldn't tell people about Jesus. Then I met you and found out that you could if people asked you, because of your role as chaplain. Jesus had prepared someone else for the job instead of me.' But I found that Janice had been in the background preparing people's hearts in that home for God to work in them. During the pandemic, she had a bright idea. She started a Sunday Club, because no one was allowed to go to church during that time. She invited every resident in the house, and the staff, and she led hymns and prayers, readings, talks and discussions. What was truly remarkable was that everyone (including those who had never been to church) came of their own free will and heard the gospel story. How much has a praying ninety-year-old got to teach us!

Prayer moves people

Nowadays, in most public places and jobs, there are rules about what you can communicate about your religion, but no one can stop you praying. If you need to stay in your room and want to offer the gift of 'helps', you can do no better than to pray for others. 'Learn to move man, through God, by prayer alone', said the famous missionary Hudson Taylor, and the Holy Spirit will take our prayers and make them effective in the lives of others.[34] If people's curiosity is aroused by your faith, or if their deepest needs make them seek you out and ask questions, there will be plenty of opportunities to share Jesus with others.

Before he was admitted to hospital with a terminal illness, a man asked to see me.

'Don't think that you're going to convert me!' he challenged me quite belligerently.

'I'm not offering to convert you,' I replied, 'because I couldn't anyway. I'm offering to pray for you.'

'Ah!' he grunted in a relieved way. 'That's alright, then.'

What was the result of that prayer? I have no idea. I can only leave it in the Lord's hands.

Regular and consistent prayer

The Bible advocates regular and consistent prayer. Indeed, the Orthodox Jewish habit was and is to pray three times a day. As I lived and worked in the Jewish community in Manchester for a number of years, I know how important this habit of prayer is for them. During the exile of the Jews to Babylon, Daniel insisted on praying in 'his upstairs room where the windows opened towards Jerusalem. Three times a day he got down on his knees and prayed, giving thanks to his God, just as he had done before' (Daniel 6:10). He was not afraid of anyone's reaction: he was only afraid of disobeying God.

---

[34] James Hudson Taylor (1832-1905) was a British missionary to China and the founder of the China Inland Mission, www.quotefancy.com/q uote/1491424/James-Hudson-Taylor-Learn-to-move-man-through-God-by-prayer-alone (accessed 5th December 2024).

Regular and consistent prayer is a wonderful habit to cultivate, and we can practise it in the 'slow lane' of life. The higher, more liturgical traditions of the Church have much to teach those of us who are evangelicals in this sphere. Liturgical rather than extempore prayer is often easier for those who have already slowed down in life, which is why the older forms of service are more attractive to older Anglicans.

Christians in churches often talk a lot about prayer, but prayer meetings are usually the most neglected of all the services. I am glad to belong to a church which takes prayer seriously. It offers lots of different time slots and a variety of prayer traditions. And, most importantly, it has the desired effect! Prayer is answered.

At the moment we have a series of teaching and leaflets called 'the rhythm of life', when we are being encouraged to pick up good spiritual habits.[35] Those of us who are older can easily get lazy about this and need to be kept on our toes. Paul reminds me that I should be praying continuously.[36] I think this means that our lives should be wrapped round with prayer, rather than meaning it is the only way we speak. If I have a negative thought about someone, I try immediately to counteract it with a positive prayer for the person's wellbeing. The moment I hear about a need, I try to pray about it. I know people who use items on the news to help them pray. For a person who has the gift of 'helps', the opportunity to pray will often lead

---

[35] Rhythm of Life is being proposed by the Diocese of Bristol, see www.bristol.anglican.org/churchlife/resourcesforparishes/rhythm-of-life (accessed 19th December 2024).

[36] 1 Thessalonians 5:17.

them to do something to help practically. The Holy Spirit will lead them first in prayer and then to be involved in a more practical way.

We will always find excuses for not praying, I remember an elderly and godly man in a church I went to in Essex when we were first married. He told me that it was always easier to go to the paper shop, buy his daily paper and then settle back to read it at home with his coffee, rather than giving himself to prayer. It was too much like hard work. At that point in my life, I didn't really understand what he was talking about. Now I do! It's so easy to be distracted in our spiritual life by the insignificant duties of the everyday. But routine prayer stands us in good stead.

I have a regular notebook which I use for my prayer requests for others. It keeps me concentrating on the job in hand. I write down the answers as well, and looking back at those answers encourages me in my prayer life.

The big dramas of prayer

In the Bible we meet quite a few 'giants of prayer', who get involved in amazing feats for God. Just think about Elijah, praying for rain to be withdrawn in 1 Kings 17:1; praying to give miraculous sustenance to a widow in 1 Kings 17:14; praying for a child to be raised from the dead in 1 Kings 17:21-22; and for rain to be restored to a whole country in 1 Kings 18:41-45. That is definitely out of our league, we might think. And yet, James reminds us, 'Elijah was a man just like us' (James 5:17, NIV 1984).

I would like to suggest that the way Elijah prayed in these dramatic situations wasn't 'just like us', but rather that he started out as a human being 'just like us'. He learned how to practise prayer, and the more he prayed, the more he saw God at work, and the more he saw God at work, the more he prayed, and so the cycle went on. I know that I am unlikely to be part of Elijah-like prayers, but I can move on in my prayer life to prove God's faithfulness more and more.

Pioneer missionary prayer

When Christian workers, both from overseas and indigenous people, witness amazing things happen in countries that have very little Christian background, it is usually through a series of people who have planted the seed through prayer. Some of those people have prayed and gone to work in the country (either supported by churches or earning their own living). Some of them have been born in the country, come to know Christ and prayed. And some of them have been the 'little people', often older and lonely, who have battled with the principalities and powers of this world in prayer.[37] Any of us can be those 'little people' who have the ministry of prayer which supports the pioneers who are out there. It is easy to become part of a regular prayer meeting for Missionary Aviation Fellowship or Open Doors or similar organisations, and we can pray in an informed and useful way.[38]

---

[37] Ephesians 6:12.
[38] Missionary Aviation Fellowship (MAF) transports doctors, other personal and provisions to locations that cannot otherwise be safely reached, www.maf-uk.org (accessed 5th December 2024); Open Doors is a non-denominational mission that supports persecuted Christians, founded by Brother Andrew in 1955, www.opendoorsuk.org (accessed 21st January 2025).

Through my life experience, I have read about and met a number of people who have been involved in the church in Algeria. In the early twentieth century there were pioneers who went there, suffered huge deprivation, saw very few results, and yet persevered and prayed. Two of them, sisters, the Misses Dudgeon, came to live in their retirement in the town where I was brought up in Kent.[39] They had given all their lives to difficult and isolated work in Algeria. I still remember them saying to me as an eleven-year-old, 'But we want our best work for the Lord to be now in our retirement.' I was impressed by what they said. I might have thought that they would be tired or think that they had done enough for the Lord over the years, but that wasn't their attitude. They used their remaining years to talk to others in England about the Lord, and to pray for the country where they had laboured – a completely unglamorous life, with very few visible results. What a witness to the gifts of missionary apostles and the small, out of the way gift of prayer in the 'slow lane' of life.

National church leaders in difficult countries need our prayer

I think of the leaders of the present-day Algerian church who were converted as the result of this early witness. I have been privileged to be on national summer camps with them and to receive their prayer letters. What an

---

[39] Miss Dorothea Dudgeon – birthdate unknown. Died 19th August 1980 in Tunbridge Wells, Kent. Miss Suzanne Dudgeon – birthdate probably 1893. Died in 1988. Both were missionaries in Algeria from before 1923 and retired in 1970. Information from the Special Archives, Manchester University (with kind permission).

example of every type of prayer they have given me! They organise regular half-nights of prayer in the church there. They encourage prayer for national revival and the Lord's guidance for their everyday lives. They pray for Algerian Christians to be sent out to other countries in North Africa and the Middle East, without any trappings of organisations, but backed up by the Church's prayer. Wow! What a witness! I can't compete with that boldness and strength. I'm only a 'little person' in the 'slow lane' of life. But I can pray with them and for them. That is the privilege that has been granted to me.

The encouragement of prayer goes full circle

Last night I was feeling discouraged with lack of achievement and restrictions because of illness in our household and the duties of caring. Then suddenly came a phone call. It was from a man in his late thirties who we knew from our years in Manchester. He had been at our church and had suffered considerably with personal challenges. My husband and I had spent a lot of time with him, praying, reading the Bible and offering practical support. After an email which explained all that God was now doing in his life, including his restored relationships and opportunities to be used in the church with his gifts, and telling us how he felt that God was helping him, he phoned to say, 'Thank you for all the times you have supported me and prayed for me over the years. It's meant so much. I also want to say how sorry I am that you are now coping with illness. I want to pray for you.'

Someone we have prayed for in the past is now praying for us. It stops us feeling that we are the strong church leaders who pray for others. When we are weak, God uses others to pray for us. It is a joy, and it is humbling, and it makes us praise God.

Think about! *Reflections on Bible passages and your own walk with the Lord*

1. What are the most significant verses of Ephesians 6:10-19 for you? Which parts of the armour of God have been essential for you in your walk with the Lord?
2. Who do you think are the key pray-ers in your family?
3. In what variety of ways could we all look for 'a better country – a heavenly one' (Hebrews 11:16) to come? Can we look for some aspects of it now?

Think about! *Your own gifts and ministry*

1. What do you think is your main role, either in your older years or in the times when you are forced by circumstances to be less active?
2. What special roles do people who are retired have in your church? Would you ever aspire to be like them?
3. What is your 'rhythm of life' or pattern of prayer? Would you ever consider introducing more variety into your prayer life?

8
Ambition and self-absorption

Bible characters

Ambition is a relentless taskmaster. There is always another goal on the horizon, and the person who is consumed by ambition is never satisfied and does not experience empathy for others. We see this characteristic clearly in the early life of Paul. He was delighted to be at the stoning of Stephen. Later, as he started out on a new venture, he was 'still breathing out murderous threats against the Lord's disciples' (Acts 9:1). His ambition was to follow God's laws and to be a focused and dedicated persecutor of Christians. He was understandably proud of all his achievements: 'If someone else thinks they have reasons to put confidence in the flesh, I have more' (Philippians 3:4).

However, Paul's goals were completely changed after his conversion. He went on to consider all the advantages he had boasted about to be as 'rubbish, that I may gain Christ' (Philippians 3:8, NKJV). This change of attitude also meant that he was not impressed by any other Christian leaders who might think that they were important: 'whatever they were makes no difference to me' (Galatians 2:6).

Yet, in that being ambitious means that we are fully focused on a goal and on the end result of our activities, Paul's ambitious character remained intact. In Philippians 3:13-14 he wrote, 'One thing I do: forgetting what is behind and straining towards what is ahead, I press on towards the goal to win the prize for which God has called me heavenwards in Christ Jesus.' Paul transposed his complete determination to succeed into the service of Jesus Christ. He often used the imagery of fights and battles and races, where there has to be a winner.[40] He used his foundational character trait for something that was supremely worthwhile. However dangerous ambition can be (and it has the potential to be very dangerous), it can be disciplined, changed from being self-seeking and of great use in the kingdom of God. Many Christian leaders have used their tendency to ambition for good purposes.

The next Bible character I would like to briefly examine combined ambition and self-absorption in his early life. That's quite an unattractive combination! Joseph was like that, partly because his father spoiled him outrageously and let him think that he had the right to show off about his superiority. He made himself very unpopular by snitching on his brothers: 'he brought their father a bad report about them' (Genesis 37:2). Like many people who are self-absorbed, he seemed totally unaware of how unpopular he had become. It provoked his brothers' jealousy, as overweening confidence in success and self-centredness always will. It doesn't matter whether it's a political or social or religious leader who demonstrates

---

[40] See, for example, 2 Timothy 4:7.

these traits, they will annoy everyone else and create enemies.

But out of this detestable arrogance, after being taken away as a slave to Egypt, Joseph led a remarkable life. His natural ambition showed in his desire to work hard and to do well. He had extraordinary success as a slave in Potiphar's household,[41] and later in prison, when he was put 'in charge of all those held in the prison' (Genesis 39:22). His natural talents came out in his ability to organise, oversee others and bring enormous financial profit for Egypt. He rose to become the Prime Minister of that country.

As God took him through the maelstrom of temptation, injustice and opportunity, Joseph changed from being an unemotional narcissist to being a man who was moved to tears at his father's and brothers' suffering. 'Deeply moved at the sight of his brother, Joseph hurried out and looked for a place to weep' (Genesis 43:30). This marks out a man whose ambition and ability have been used by God, but whose self-absorption and desire for revenge have been totally turned around. He was able to say to the brothers who wronged him and nearly had him killed, 'Do not be distressed … because it was to save lives that God sent me ahead of you' (Genesis 45:5). He became an important part of God's plan for the future, his influence felt for generations to come. He was no longer a spoilt, self-absorbed and arrogant teenager.

---

[41] Genesis 39:2-6.

Understanding why God chooses to use us

One day, many years ago, I had the privilege of listening to a live talk by a famous Israeli leader. One of his points was that the world was fortunate to have the Jews because they were so talented and brilliant. While that is partly true, I wanted to point him to a verse in the Bible that tells something completely different. Deuteronomy 7:7-8 tells us, 'The LORD did not set his affection on you and choose you because you were more numerous than other peoples, for you were the fewest of all peoples. But it was because the LORD loved you.' God's desire to bless the Jewish people and us is because of His love, not because of our gifts. If we are to be used by God either in the more dramatic stories of His work or in the 'slow lane' of life, where many of us are, we can be ambitious for the values of God's kingdom, but we cannot exhibit the self-absorption which is the complete opposite of Christlikeness.

Questions we might like to ask ourselves

There are some questions we need to ask ourselves about ambition and self-absorption, so we can either get rid of them or put them in their rightful place.

When it comes to ambition, is this inevitable for someone who is young and full of energy, who wants to use their skills in a worthwhile cause? Does the pursuit of ambition give us enough time to slow down, or will we inevitably be working and driving ourselves helter-skelter to success?

Can life with Jesus overcome the need for ambition, or does it just get subverted into something else? Or is

Christianity only for those who don't have much drive or get up and go? Could we have spiritual ambition, follow the route of pride and so follow Satan's sin of rebellion?

Finding our role in church

I heard a speaker once suggest that Christians who hadn't achieved much in their career were more tempted than others to be spiritually ambitious and even show off about their spiritual achievements. That immediately struck me as making sense. It is so easy to compensate for our perceived inadequacies by trying to look 'big' in a church setting.

However, we must be careful not to be too cynical, because there are a lot of people who put energy into organising things for church and who feel a sense of fulfilment in doing this. And church leaders are very grateful to all those who give so much time and energy to God's people. I guess we have to make sure that our motivation is about serving God, not about being number one, and we must not be annoyed when we are not acknowledged.

There have been many Christian women (it has applied predominantly to women because of fewer opportunities for them in the workplace) in previous generations who haven't been able to pursue a career, but who have been able to organise Sunday schools, women's meetings and provide refreshments for church celebrations. It's very useful to have people with those sorts of skills and, with so many people now working full-time, it can be quite hard to find enough volunteers to do these jobs. That's where men and women of retirement age can find fulfilment in practising the gift of 'helps'. In my church there is a veritable army of retirees who support functions as volunteers, using their many gifts. The danger is that frustrated volunteers who have been denied job satisfaction will try to manage and exercise authority over everyone else.

I had a lady in one church who would never contribute to the sandwiches for a church tea, even though she was brilliant at the job, because she did not want to be part of a group who made big doorstep sandwiches with unappetising crusts. It was her pride which stopped her because she didn't want to be classed in the same way as those who had no culinary skills. As a result, we all lost out!

It's great to use our God-given skills, whether or not they have been recognised in a secular sphere. I had a young lady in one of my churches who was a nurse but who had always wanted to be a primary school teacher as well. She became a very fulfilled Sunday school teacher and organiser of young children, and she went on extra training courses run by the Diocese. She ended up combining both jobs – professional and voluntary – extremely successfully.

On the other hand, as mentioned, there is a danger that we will use those skills to seem important and to rule over other people. That is not the way of Christ. We are to be submissive to one another – a command given 'out of reverence for Christ' (Ephesians 5:21) which is often forgotten and doesn't just refer to the relationship between men and women or between husbands and wives. If we all concentrated on being submissive to one another, there wouldn't be so many problems in the Church.

It is also natural for those who are very able in the secular sphere to gain automatic recognition in a church. How many business leaders, doctors and teachers do you have among your elders? This can lead to two dangers. We can either show too much respect to those we might see as our social superiors (doffing our caps) or, if we are part of that group, we can easily take our own sense of superiority into church. Who can forget the pews in Church of England buildings that were specially reserved for the local gentry? We might mock that idea in the twenty-first century, but there are plenty of modern parallels. We must beware of those tendencies. We should go into God's presence as equals and not look for social recognition.

Non-conformist churches need not be proud of having avoided this problem either. In the church where I grew up, we all sat in a circle, but we all understood who were socially 'superior' to others, and even as children we knew who those people were. Snobbery enters churches only too easily.

Accepting those who are misfits socially

Congregations can make an effort to acknowledge difficult or even eccentric people, and it takes everyone out of their comfort zone. It will involve spending time with people we do not naturally get on with. We might invite someone to the church evening service, but what about inviting them to supper afterwards? It's easy to say that we should, but we don't always naturally enjoy it or feel at ease doing it. After all, it might involve spending less time chatting with our friends.

It's one of the big problems of after-church socialising, and it's why churches often get accused of having cliques.

We'd rather keep going with our 'in-house' conversations than make room for someone else. Usually, the one who successfully joins the group is the one who is placid and easily agrees with everyone else.

But making everyone feel comfortable is not as easy as it sounds. It's the way of the cross and we don't like it. I was so proud of a church I was involved in when they coped with a lady who had serious problems with personal hygiene. Several of my congregation made a real effort to include her in their group.

Sometimes we need to be creative and realistic in the way in which we deal with such problems. We came to the point where we wanted to make this lady feel welcome at one of our home groups. The hostess and I discussed what to do. We decided that soft furnishings were going to be the ones which were most at risk in this situation, and the hostess was very worried about her husband's reaction because he wasn't part of the group, or a believer. We made the decision that the hard dining chairs were the ones that could be best adapted to the situation, and so I made sure I arrived a bit early, sat on one of the hard chairs and invited the lady to sit next to me the moment she arrived. It worked brilliantly! She felt welcome but we didn't ignore the reservations of the host, and air freshener was always in liberal supply! Another member of the congregation found her extra clothes, and another invited her to share Christmas with her family

How should we cope with our differences?

Should I acknowledge that I am different from others? I find for myself that I am happy to mix with the poor, but what about my mixing with those who don't read or never stop talking? Or whom I find just plain boring? This is why living with people who are different is so costly. I admire those who live sacrificially, whose door is always open to others, like young people from the Eden teams who form part of The Message outreach, for example.[42] For me, living in a poor housing area is not difficult at all. That's been part of my experience for a number of years. I find living in an area where there is a lot of crime is doable. By contrast, living with people who only watch TV or listen to loud music is hard. The only way I can think of doing it is to have a rota for open homes or a community centre so that those who need constant support from others will always have somewhere to go.

I think about Mia, a member of our youth group. She was a needy young person who had experienced very little love in her background. In the end, three of us took two days each week to reply to her constant text messages, so that one person didn't have to be on the job continually. Most of the time she just needed reassurance, but it was a relief to know that it was only your turn for two days a week.

I remember how humbled my family felt when she came to sleep at our house for a few days at Christmas. It was a very ordinary family Christmas, with stockings in the morning and people at the house for Christmas dinner. When she left three days later, she thanked us for the way we had made her feel welcome. 'That is the most amazing

---

[42] Eden teams started working in Manchester in 1997 as part of the outreach of The Message Trust, a Christian charity working among young people. It was founded in 1988 by Andy Hawthorne, www.message.org.uk (accessed 5th December 2024).

Christmas I have ever had,' she said, with genuine appreciation. We had Christmases like that every year. For her it was a revelation to have ordinary family around her, rather than family who were intent on manipulating her or pushing drugs on to her.

How would living continually with someone like Mia work, especially if you needed time to study or be quiet? It's a matter of knowing what is right for you and what God has called you to, to know how to minister to someone in a self-sacrificial way without being a doormat or denying who you really are. I guess if we bring all our callings to the Lord, He will show us how to navigate the needs of others, even when we feel inadequate.

Once, when I was doing a lay reader's course, I had the opportunity to take a work colleague to an Alpha course. At first I thought I was just too busy to go. Then I thought, what an irony! I want to be used in the ministry, but training was going to make me too busy to help a genuine seeker. I decided that there was no reason not to accompany my colleague, with the result that they became a Christian, and I found that God gave me all the time I needed to study. That took a step of faith, because job and family commitments were demanding, and it would have been easy to find excuses not to go.

Finding our own calling in the way of the cross

We are all called to live the way of the cross – all of us, not just those of us who have spiritual ambition or want to be church leaders. When Christian leaders turn their backs on the world, they must be primarily motivated by love. They have been called to do something else instead of selfish self-seeking.

147

Ambition isn't the only human quality that has to change. When St Francis of Assisi was called to the monastic life, I assume that there were other Christian aristocrats who stayed in their traditional spheres of life while practising their faith. Francis was called to something else, and he was right to respond to God's special calling.[43] The emphasis should not be on the rejection; it should be on the calling. If I am a rich socialite and become a Christian, I should spend time serving other people in love and not automatically abandon my place of influence, unless God asks me to. Think about famous footballers who become Christians and the influence they have on young people!

The main motivation for all callings must be love. I think of a nun who told the story of her calling on a TV programme. Although she had fallen in love with a man and that love was reciprocated, she felt it wasn't enough for her. Her love for Jesus was more all-consuming. The greatness of the divine love stopped the renunciation of a human love being a hardship or an impossible sacrifice. She felt joyful about it.

When we turn to Christ, we gain a different perspective. From then on, we see everything in the light of eternity. When I became a Christian, my ambition became a greater one. It was about what I wanted to achieve for a greater purpose: seeing people come to faith who would be with God for eternity; seeing people helped and loved who would experience Christ more closely as a result of what I would do; having the privilege of helping

---

[43] St Francis of Assisi (c 1181–1226) was a renowned Italian Christian monk and mystic.

people who had nothing for the sake of Christ; being one of the 'little people' who could use the gift of 'helps' to draw alongside others. What is the point, asks Jesus in the Gospel of Matthew 16:26, of gaining the whole world and losing your soul? The answer is that there is no point. And in the end, what we choose will affect our happiness and fulfilment. 'He is no fool', said Jim Elliot, 'who gives what he cannot keep [his life] to gain that which he cannot lose [eternal life].'[44] He lived out his beliefs to the very end!

On a recent TV documentary about his life, Volodymyr Zelenskyy, the president of Ukraine, talking about the sacrifices he has made to lead his people in time of war, said, 'You have to make a choice. What is the price of your life?'[45] It is interesting that a secular but highly principled leader uses the same terminology as Jesus to explain why he has taken on the hugely sacrificial task of leading his country.

Jim Elliot's words make sense. The challenge for all of us is to act as though it really does make sense. When you become a Christian, you have to take a step along the path which leads to eternal life, and no one knows what that first step might lead to. Only God knows, and that is where faith comes in. Sometimes the reality of that choice will hit us hard. But we go on regardless!

---

[44] Jim Elliot (1927–56) was a missionary to the Auca people of South America,
www.goodreads.com/author/quotes/2125255.Jim_Elliot#:~:text=He%20is%20no%20fool%20who,that%20which%20he%20cannot%20lose (accessed 5th December 2024).
[45] *The Zelensky Story*, www.bbc.co.uk/programmes/m001zps2 (accessed 5th December 2024).

If God chooses to call me to work with those whom the world despises in a deprived parish, or with elderly, forgotten people in care homes, or with socially isolated people in tower blocks, who am I to reject the calling? Especially as the One who calls me gave everything for me in the first place. 'For you know the grace of our Lord Jesus Christ, that though he was rich, yet for your sake he became poor, so that you through his poverty might become rich' (2 Corinthians 8:9).

If we reject self-absorption, which is empty and achieves nothing, we can be ambitious to see the kingdom of God expand and to hear the words, 'Well done, good and faithful servant!' (Matthew 25:23). We can follow the calling we are given because we can trust the wisdom of the One who calls in love and who knows what's best for us.

Think about! *Reflections on Bible passages and your own walk with the Lord*

1. Do you find anything humanly difficult in Paul's character as revealed in the New Testament, or do you find yourself feeling total admiration for him?
2. Are there Christian leaders you find irritating or difficult to admire? How do you cope with these emotions?
3. Have you ever given up a comfortable lifestyle, or even some comforts, to serve Christ? Did it turn out to be worthwhile in terms of ministry?

Think about! *Your own gifts and ministry*

1. Have you ever had anyone come to your church whom people have found difficult to accept socially? How did you cope with the situation?
2. What sort of advice would you give to someone who was converted from a socially very successful background?
3. How would you pray for someone who comes from a very different background from yourself and who perhaps could resent the difference?

9
Discipline

Jeremiah's experience

Jeremiah 10:23-24 says:

> I know, O LORD, that a man's life is not his own;
> it is not for man to direct his steps.
> Correct me, LORD, but only with justice –
> not in your anger,
> lest you reduce me to nothing.
> (NIV 1984)

What an amazing couple of verses to find in my daily readings in Jeremiah! They contain so many truths in a couple of short verses, and they give us teaching about God's direction of our lives.

Jeremiah knew from deep personal experience that his life and his destiny were not his own. Jeremiah 1:5 tells us that God had chosen him while he was 'in the womb'. While we can choose to cooperate with Him, God has the ultimate say in our destiny. That is not the same as believing in the Greek fates, and we must bear in mind that we have free choice. Oh dear! What a pickle! I'm not getting into that one for too long! It's bound to end badly!

These verses are not about predestination, which as a theoretical doctrine can seem so relentless and stultifying, because in chapter 10 verse 24, Jeremiah asks God to correct him, and if someone is bound by an inexorable fate, then correction wouldn't make any difference. If you want to understand that, read about the example of Oedipus in the Greek tragedy.[46] He did his best to avoid his prophesied fate but still ended up killing his father and marrying his mother in an incestuous relationship. Lots of doom-laden destiny going on there!

Jeremiah doesn't want to be put through the mill of God's anger, because God's anger is real and is totally justifiable as it is a reaction of God's holiness towards humanity's sinfulness. If that were to happen, says Jeremiah, he might be reduced 'to nothing' – either literally disintegrate or have no self-worth at all (v24). This is an important point and should always be borne in mind when we are considering Paul's statement about being the 'chief' of sinners (1 Timothy 1:15, NKJV). We may be the chief of sinners (whatever that means – are we talking about persecuting Christians, being a Hitler or being full of pride and vanity? You can decide on that one). However bad we may feel we have been, it does not mean we are worth nothing. Eastern religions may not lay much worth on the individual, but Christianity does. Jeremiah asks God to correct him, not to wipe him out. God needs to correct us, not because He is cruel, but so that we will display the truth of the gospel, the beauty of Jesus and the compassionate love of the cross.

If we are not corrected by God, we will become vainer and probably be more proudly religious which, let's face

---

[46] Sophocles, *Oedipus Rex*, Greek tragedy first performed in Athens in 429 BC.

it, is not a turn-on for others, and we will certainly not fulfil our destiny, which is to become more like Jesus. Our job or place in the religious hierarchy seems to be less important than the transformation of our personalities.

How did Moses manage to be one of the greatest leaders of all time and yet be the humblest man on the earth?[47] I don't know, but God seems to have taken him firmly in hand.

The purpose of discipline and the link with correction

Correction and discipline aren't exactly the same thing. Correction has more the feel of being put right quite decisively and of being a one-off action after you have been in trouble. Discipline has more the feel of being nudged, made to think about your lifestyle, and shown the way through adverse circumstances, which makes it character building. But the two are certainly strongly linked. And Jeremiah is desperate enough to ask to be corrected.

If you're anything like me, you want to avoid discipline, never mind correction. I always hated those red marks on the pages of my exercise book in school. 'Why did the teacher not appreciate my brilliance rather than wasting ink on putting me right?' I would ask myself. Sometimes I was so embarrassed by the bad mark that I refused to read the accompanying remarks. Now, you may say that I was an arrogant little so-and-so, but my experience as a teacher was that 98 per cent of my pupils felt the same way about my own red marking pen. They generally ignored my corrections and advice and carried on with what they had

---

[47] Numbers 12:3.

always done. It was only after several repetitions of comments and a personal conversation with them that they started to take some notice, usually after something like parents' evening.

My experiences of Christian discipline are set against my squirming, rebellious, know-it-all character. I'm only discussing it here because experience tells me that I can't avoid it and stay in the game of the Christian life. And I certainly couldn't be used in the slow lane of life with the gift of 'helps'.

Discipline as part of being a follower

Discipline has the same linguistic root as the word 'disciple', and that's what Jesus' followers were called. It's not a word which has been chosen by chance. It has to do with what it means to be a follower. Following Jesus is not the same as being a fan, or an Instagram follower, or posting a 'like' after a Facebook post. It is about a whole life turnaround, which is the meaning of the word 'conversion'. It's not enough to learn and approve of a Jesus theology. You have to wade in there with your wellington boots on, and it's not even just a gut reaction when you are crying out for God's help. Keeping going as a disciple takes discipline.

How unfashionable that is. What I remember about teaching exam classes at secondary school is that pupils want teachers to give them the right answers so that they can do well. It is all about the end product, not the ongoing hard process. They often don't want to think because that takes serious brain work and energy. 'It's solid, Miss,' as my cleverest student used to say about understanding the philosophy of Wordsworth in his poetry. That pupil was clever enough to recognise how hard it was to understand the depths of Wordsworth's poetry. Most pupils don't want to have their weaknesses or lack of understanding exposed. It's too humiliating. It's too painful, too tiring and, worst of all, they fear failure. All that pain is not worth it if you can't be sure of success.

Jesus says the opposite. He says the pain is worth it because it's going to transform you, even if you don't look like a more successful Christian, or get a better job, or get chosen as an elder of your church. He says that no one else might see the result, but it's still worth it, because God rewards 'those who diligently seek Him' (Hebrews 11:6, NKJV).

We laugh at the Pharisees who used long prayers or wore extra-wide phylacteries to impress, because we can see through those hypocritical habits so easily. In truth, it's very easy to see through the hypocrisies of other people's religion, but we're easily blinded to our own. It's hard to refuse to spread gossip, answer back or reject an unjust accusation from a colleague when we are only doing it to please God, rather than seeking other people's admiration. In theory we agree with the biblical principle that He 'who sees what is done in secret, will reward you' (Matthew 6:4). But really believing it and putting it into practice is much harder.

Those who endure trials

I am full of admiration for people who are prisoners of conscience especially when they are not Christians. They do it for the greater good and because they believe in justice. There's a woman in Iran who is frequently being placed into solitary confinement in Evin Prison in Tehran because she is continually speaking out about its horrors, and she won't be silent.[48] She believes in something greater than herself. How noble!

I am full of admiration for many of the housekeepers who work in sheltered housing units. They go out of their way to take extra care of their residents, working longer hours than they are paid for, visiting residents in hospital and finding out what is good for them. They don't boast about it, but I see them doing this work in the most unselfish ways possible. That is also true for many care workers who are loving and considerate towards those under their charge. I feel humbled by the way that they assume this is normal and they don't ask for any extra recognition. And, of course, voluntary carers in our society do even more out of love rather than for payment. This is what God is asking us to do when we offer the gift of 'helps'.

Discipline comes from love

But Jesus doesn't ask us to do this because we're noble. He asks us to do it in response to the love that drove Him to the cross. We're not being asked to sign up for a great self-disciplining, self-improvement movement. We're being asked to take part in a greater 'in love' movement.

Discipline by itself can make us hard and inflexible. Some of us are more tempted by it than others. If you like beating yourself up physically or psychologically, you probably like the idea of discipline. Suppose that you are madly in love with someone and you want to be with them

---

[48] Narges Mohammadi, deputy head of Defenders of Human Rights Center, currently in Evin Prison, Tehran.

all the time. Then they are offered the opportunity to undergo some training elsewhere. They love their job, and you know it will do them good. Instead of staying at home and moping, you let them go willingly and use the time apart well. Love makes you both selfish – you want to hang on to the loved one 24/7 – and unselfish – you care more about their fulfilment than your own convenience.

In the same way, discipline is based on love. And it's also based on faith. Those who come to God, says Hebrews 11:6, 'must believe that he exists' – not just an intellectual exercise – 'and that he rewards those who earnestly seek him'. It's not just the big decisions of life which reveal that mindset. It's the little day-to-day decisions – not to bad-mouth someone, not to gain promotion by pulling someone else down, doing the chores when you'd rather sit by the fire and enjoy the conversation. A decision to be Christlike is a decision of faith, because everything in our culture and human nature runs counter to it.

I have to confess that I've always been like my former students. If I could take a shortcut in language work, I would do so. I would prefer to pretend that I was talented in some area of learning than work to achieve it. Years of pretence and cheating actually made me rather good at working out when my pupils were doing just that! I was always one step ahead of them!

How to avoid discipline

Of course, it helps if you have money. I remember a pupil saying that they didn't need help with their examination coursework because their private tutor would help them do exactly what was needed. Except that they didn't.

Although the tutor found a perfect subject analysis on the internet, it didn't do what the exam marking scheme asked the student to do and could be discovered far too easily.

There's only so far you can cheat before disaster raises its head. And even if you succeed in such a way at 'A' level, you still have to cope with university exams. But universities are finding that there are more and more students who will pay to get their coursework written for them. A colleague from a different academic discipline, who was particularly brilliant, was frequently approached by former students once they had gone to university, wanting their essays to be written for them. A more impersonal approach is to get the internet to do it for you. And the advent of Artificial Intelligence is only going to make this problem worse.

University lecturers are often at the receiving end of harassment when it comes to awarding grades. Some more-openly corrupt societies in different countries have had to cope with this for years – literally money being paid for academic certificates. Sadly, we could be approaching that situation here in the UK if we are not careful.

'So whose writing is this?' I asked one of my students as I looked over their university entrance application (UCAS) personal statement. The student readily admitted it was the work of a relative who was a professional. I pointed out that the people who would be reading personal statements written by teenagers might suspect that the work wasn't theirs! My student didn't care because they thought it was the best, and 'the best' would get them a university place!

It starts at primary school. I remember the painted Easter egg competition at my children's infant school. It wasn't a competition between the children; it was one that tested the ingenuity of the parents. As I have no gifts in that direction, I more or less condemned my children to failure in the annual egg-painting competition. They seem to have survived the experience!

For years at school, I enjoyed reading English translations of classical literature, but I found it a lot harder to get down to learning the rules for irregular verbs in Latin and Greek. It was a timely failure and helped me to change my attitude to learning. It was failing an important exam in translation (and I prided myself on never failing exams) that turned my attitude around and helped me to face reality.

When I received the result, I felt profoundly depressed. I had to face the fact that I wasn't a top student, when I had been deceiving myself that I was. Feeling downcast, I talked to my father. 'I'm not a top achiever either,' he admitted, 'and I always found that disappointing.' I knew he found it hard to say that, because he had always been aiming for the top position in his job. I admired his honesty. I didn't feel any less depressed about my exam mark after that conversation, but at least my father wasn't trying to make it alright by reassuring me that I could be top if I wanted it badly enough. It was the meeting of real minds, and I appreciated it.

From that bottom place of despair, I learned bit by bit that I had to work hard just to be 'good enough', even though it probably meant I wouldn't be top. The first thing to nail was those impossible Greek verb systems. After six weeks of learning and relearning, I started to rise up to the middle of the class. Rather than feeling despairing, I felt quite proud of being mediocre.

I had to learn the same lesson over and over again in all areas of life, and each time it was hard. I enjoyed writing English Literature essays at university, but then I found I wanted to take shortcuts in the preparation. As a young Christian, God spoke to me through Colossians 3:17: 'And whatever you do, whether in word or deed, do it all in the name of the Lord Jesus, giving thanks to God the Father through him.' I knew that meant I had to do the preparatory reading thoroughly and not cheat by looking at someone else's notes.

I have found throughout my life that I have fought the same temptations over and over again. When I became a teacher, I loved my job, but I wanted to take shortcuts in filling out my mark book or completing the estimated grade sheets. I was certainly in need of the Lord's discipline!

Looking at success in a new light

One of my temptations was always wanting to do something that was 'more important' than what I was doing at that particular time. How about being married to a successful Christian leader, or being a missionary in a difficult country, or writing a novel? Anything that would take me away from the humdrum of the here and now! It took me a long time to realise that it might be enough to be 'a good teacher'. When I was a vicar, I found the temptation was always to want to be in with 'the right people' or 'the successful evangelicals'.

And so we come again to the question of the gift of 'helps' and working in the slow lane of life. Perhaps God's discipline will help us to acknowledge that we need to accept the job God has given us to do, even if it doesn't seem very glamorous. That's been a real eye-opener for me!

What would have happened if God had called me to work with the people who had major mental health problems, or who didn't know about the latest fashionable Christian music, or who didn't have amazing testimonies to share? Was I willing to do that for the kingdom?

When I came to work as a chaplain with older people in a secular business environment, I had to learn the lesson all over again. I'm a slow learner in this area of life! I had lots of experience in helping older people, but very few people in the management area of the business consulted me. They wanted to use the PR department and the media department and the HR department instead of me. A chaplain, I found, was worthy of very little consideration when it came to business success. But in this sort of situation, we need to ask ourselves, what does God consider worthy of consideration?

What if God had called me to listen to older people who were in trouble, or to pray with those who were seeking Him? Time and again the elderly people who were being housed and cared for and those who were caring for them on the front line asked for my help. In my pride I found I wanted acknowledgement from those who were considered to be important by the business hierarchy. 'If only they knew how much I had to offer them,' I thought! It revealed an arrogance of which I am now completely ashamed.

Working at the coal face of Christian ministry is not glamorous and we are very often 'passed by' by those who know what it means to be successful. Christian outreach groups would rather have someone to speak who is an 'influencer' than someone who is struggling to follow God. A converted pop singer or TV personality would always be the speaker of choice rather than someone from a humbler position.

In the same way, I remember hearing a speaker who, at a public meeting, told us about his amazing conversion (it seemed genuine) and then about how God had healed him of so many problems instantly, such as his episodes of schizophrenia. I was pleased that he had been released from this most burdensome of problems, but I also winced for those listening who might be continuing to suffer with mental health problems and had not experienced the 'miracle cure'. It can take a huge amount of faith and perseverance to visit the mental health unit regularly, take medication daily, discover that it is difficult to carry out an ordinary job properly and still praise God for His goodness. For those people who were suffering – and several of them were members of my church – I wanted a testimony of someone who had discovered Jesus in the daily cost of faithful Christian living as well as those who had amazing conversion stories.

Discipline that reveals limitations as well as opportunities

Learning means discovering your own limitations, but also endeavouring to push past them. Hebrews 12:5-11 tells us that every father disciplines his child because he loves them. The practical means of parental discipline don't matter. They tend to come and go according to the fashion and the generation. But the idea of boundaries which are non-negotiable is very important.

There are boundaries which no Christian can disagree about – the Ten Commandments. But there are other boundaries which represent wisdom and good choices, and I think discipline could be about making good choices – those which help us choose a deep level of spiritual life.

Self-discipline is about readily accepting the necessity of limitations and the need to engage in rigorous work. Not being greedy for food is saying that one can accept emptiness because at the right time the stomach will be satisfied. It's about not cramming the body with quickly satisfying food, because that way there will be no room for nutritious food to do its important work. It's saying that someone else can eat first. It might be saying that someone else who goes hungry in the world can eat instead of me. Fasting is saying that instead of satisfying my physical hunger, I am going to make sure that my spiritual hunger is satisfied. Or that when I want my brother or sister to be blessed, I want that more than feeling full.

Greed, hunger and food are very important analogies for me about the way I live life. When we were going through a period of our lives when we didn't know where the next meal was coming from, it was a shock to go and work in a place where there was abundant food on offer. One way I reacted was that I wanted to overindulge when food was free. It was as if I could not trust God to provide me with the next meal at the right time.

Saying 'no', doing without for the sake of pursuing something more satisfying, has been a very hard discipline for me to learn. I always wanted to 'stuff myself' just in case God did not come up trumps. It's a lack of real trust in God, and it's because I don't think I'm worth enough.

I'd better take potluck because God might withdraw His love from me.

Trusting God because we know that He loves us

I know in theory that God loves me, and that gives me value, but I often don't appreciate it in terms of real understanding. Repeating 'because you're worth it' like the advert a million times doesn't do the job.[49] You need to know it deep inside, and sometimes you need to know it as a blind step of faith. Take 'the shield of faith', says Ephesians 6:16, 'with which you will be able to quench all the fiery darts of the wicked one' (NKJV). The fiery darts often appear to reveal that we are not good enough to cling on to the goodness of God.

In my working life I see the difference between those who go through the tragedies of life with a deep faith and those who don't. If you only have a superficial faith based on 'niceness' and church attendance, you will feel hurt and bitter. It is only when you have a foundational and deep experience of God's goodness and love that you can come to accept His will, even if you don't understand it.

I am alarmed at how young people are deluding themselves with cheap success which costs nothing. The success is ephemeral and quickly disappears. Then there is nothing left. Spiritual discipline which is necessary for young and old is not like that.

---

[49] Originally used by Ilon Specht, editor of a New York advertising agency, in 1971; now used by L'Oréal Paris.

The pleasure of real learning in life

The point of going through the pain of learning is to enjoy making progress, even when it is slow; seeing an achievement that is satisfying – how to wire the house, how to make an excellent cake, how to speak a language, how to grasp a new concept, how to master a new area of knowledge. This kind of learning is very pleasing, allows for true self-congratulation and boosts one's confidence.

In my own experience, this kind of 'true learning' took place when I went back to university to do a doctorate and learned what makes a really good piece of research, as I listened to my supervisor and put his advice into practice. I wrote and rewrote, researched different articles and differentiated between the different arguments. I found writing the footnotes incredibly hard, because I am not naturally a detail person, but very gradually the whole thing took shape. I loved being surrounded by scholars in the archives, by young, vibrant students in the communal areas, and by lecturers and postgraduate students in the local vegetarian café. I was thrilled when I was chosen to present a paper for the Ecclesiastical History Society, along with other post-graduates from across the country.[50] I had no illusions that I would have an academic career or that I was particularly talented. I just enjoyed every minute of learning, even the viva, and felt a warm glow of achieving something worthwhile.[51] Given the opportunity

---

[50] Ecclesiastical History Society (EHS) was founded in 1961 for the purposes of academic research in the UK, www.ecclesiasticalhistorysociety.com (accessed 5th December 2024).

[51] A 'viva' is an aural test in which the student is asked direct questions about their study and the conclusions they have reached. As

to pursue more academic arguments and write more articles, I found I didn't want that sort of work. It wasn't for me, but I loved the six-year experience of learning as an adult.

I've learned that I can't hurry the exercise of discipline for myself. It's the time when very often God says, 'Slow down,' and, as I submit to God, I will be slowed down whether I like it or not. The only difference about doing it willingly is that I will not be frustrated or angry and will consciously keep my ear to the ground to find out what God is saying to me. Thus, it will become a meaningful experience.

Watching our adult children learn the lessons of life

All of us worry about our children, even when they are following the Lord. Adult children also have to go through the experience of discipline, and it may be a painful one. Our instinct as parents is to try to relieve them of the problem – bright advice about how 'everything turns out alright in the end', or offering financial help to soften the blow. That is also true of young people we meet in our youth groups, many of which may come to us with their problems. I have met young women who have worried desperately about whether they would ever meet the right life partner – an anxiety I remember from my own young adulthood. If I could have clicked my fingers and found the right man for them, I would have done so. If I could have persuaded them that their careers in themselves were fulfilling and meaningful (as they often were) without the

---

they don't know what the questions are going to be, it is especially demanding.

necessity for a special relationship, I would have done so. Just standing on the sideline and witnessing anxiety, lack of self-belief and frustration is a very hard thing to do. If you're like me, you always want to solve the problem, and obviously on this occasion you can't! In fact, if you could, it would curtail the young adult's experience of discipline and trust in God. Not only is it impossible to find a life partner for someone else (suddenly we understand the cultural practice of arranged marriages!), but it takes away from the experience of trusting in God to reveal His best for us.

Discipline is not about the joys of suffering. Discipline is about becoming more like Jesus and therefore becoming more 'whole'. When a young person we knew through our youth work went through the trauma of job loss, it was upsetting. No amount of advice or easy comfort made any difference. But that same trial made the person more sensitive to other people's suffering and failures. It's called being 'conformed to [His] image' (Romans 8:29), and it's an uncomfortable process for which there are no shortcuts.

The final outcome of discipline

God doesn't put us through trials for ever. He is not intent on wiping us out. That's Satan's aim. God is interested in bringing us through to the other side and even bringing good out of the trial, though perhaps don't tell anyone that when they are personally suffering a trial, because they won't want to know!

Jeremiah is traditionally known as the prophet of doom. He was always telling Judah where they'd gone wrong and how their country was not going to be delivered from the hand of the enemy. It didn't make him popular, and there were plenty of other prophets around who prophesied 'the delusions of their own minds' (Jeremiah 23:26).

But on the back of the prophecies of doom and failure, Jeremiah had something surprising to say to the captured exiles:

> My eyes will watch over them for their good, and I will bring them back to this land. I will build them up and not tear them down; I will plant them and not uproot them. I will give them a heart to know me, that I am the LORD. They will be my people, and I will be their God, for they will return to me with all their heart.
> (Jeremiah 24:6-7)

Let's not pretend that God delivered them from defeat. He didn't. Let's not pretend that God delivered them from heartache and destitution. He didn't. But God had not forgotten His people, and He will not forget us.

I sometimes think about one of the saddest cases I knew from one of our youth groups in the past – a teenager who had never had a mother's input since the age of two and who had constantly been in different council and foster homes. What did they lack? Love and discipline. They were given adequate money by the state, but had no idea how to look after it. They deliberately sabotaged every opportunity they had. They lacked any sense of self-worth, which would have been fostered by discipline. They were always drawing attention to themselves by calling out an ambulance at night and picking quarrels with their contemporaries.

I think of another young person who had schizophrenic episodes over a long period of time and so never had the discipline which education can give. Thankfully, through family and church influence, they made tremendous progress, and their life was gradually turned around.

Discipline is saying 'no' to unhelpful things for a purpose. The purpose is to pursue the helpful things in our lives – a strong body, a balanced mental health, a pure mind, the ability to learn. We always want to give up on the discipline, to wallow in self-indulgence, which gets us nowhere. When we choose to come into God's family, He does not give up on us, and we come to appreciate His discipline.

Think about! *Reflections on Bible passages and your own walk with the Lord*

1.   What evidence is there, mainly in the book of Exodus, that Moses was 'more humble than anyone else on the face of the earth' (Numbers 12:3)? What do you think is the connection between discipline and being humble?
2.   Has God ever put you through the mill of discipline? How did you react?
3.   Do you find yourself wanting to take shortcuts to success? How do you deal with this problem?

Think about! *Your own gifts and ministry*

1.   Have you ever found yourself 'passed by' by those who are further up in the hierarchy of the church?
2.   What has been your strategy when dealing with a personal contact whom you suspect has never experienced parental discipline in their earlier life?
3.   What area of discipline do you rebel against in your own life? What is your attitude to that?

10
Death – the ultimate slowdown

The fearless and fearful in the story of Elijah

There seems to be a certain type of person – perhaps a fearless fighting warrior or explorer – who goes on eagerly facing danger regardless of the threat of death. At first sight, Elijah is someone in that category. After all, he has stood up to Ahab and Jezebel, despite all their threats. He is very different in nature to Obadiah who is nervous not only of the king and queen, but also of Elijah's demands. 'What have I done wrong,' asks Obadiah, 'that you are handing your servant over to Ahab to be put to death?' (1 Kings 18:9). I'm with Obadiah all the way. I identify with his sense of grievance as he faces possible death as a result of Elijah's bravery: 'Yet I your servant have worshipped the LORD since my youth' (18:12). In the biblical narrative, you can almost hear his desire to justify himself coming through the text.

However, Elijah doesn't stay as the stalwart, tough hero. In 1 Kings 19:3 we read, 'Elijah was afraid and ran for his life.' In verse 4, it is quite clear that he wants to die by whatever method is convenient, with possibly a desire for suicide being hinted at. 'I have had enough, LORD,' he says. 'Take my life.' In verse 10 he feels justifiably sorry for himself: 'I am the only one left, and now they are trying to kill me too.'

God does not answer Elijah by giving him reassurance about his life being preserved. Instead, he is granted an amazing experience of the Lord's presence: 'the LORD is about to pass by' (1 Kings 19:11). After this experience, Elijah faces up fearlessly to Ahab and Jezebel, and never indulges in self-pity and fear again.

When he is about to die, he says, 'the LORD has sent me to the Jordan' (2 Kings 2:6). God even sends Elisha to be his companion, and in verse 11, 'As they were walking along and talking together … Elijah went up to heaven.' This is his 'real' death, rather than the ones he has anticipated when he felt so fearful, and this should be a reassurance to us too, as we face death, with the knowledge of the Lord's presence with us.

We may not have the heroic calibre of an Elijah (or of the amazing martyrs of the faith who die through persecution today), but we know that God will take us through death, and, in our ministry in the slow lane of life, we can reassure others that this will be true for them too.

Should we keep busy to the end?

Some of us would like to keep busy right until the last moment, just as Elijah did. In many ways this is a good thing. Why not have purpose and direction right until the end? It's likely to keep us going. But if that means we never stop to think about the real meaning of life, if we never stop to wonder about mistakes we might have made or people we might have hurt, then I don't think we are doing ourselves any favours.

Many people would like to ignore the fact that they are dying. Apparently, many hospital visitors don't like seeing clergy in the corridor because it makes them think that someone must be dying. In the past, people would stop when they saw a funeral cortège, because it was a chance to show respect, remove their hats, if they were male, or make the sign of the cross. Now, we just feel annoyed that the slow speed of the cortège is holding us up. I had a Catholic priest friend who told me that it was sometimes difficult for him to visit someone to administer the last rites because the family didn't want the person who was ill to realise that they were dying. The family would rather crowd round the bed of the patient, talking about their lives and what they would be doing next. Some people in hospices choose to feel woozy on a last glass of wine so that they are not uncomfortably aware that they are dying.

If death does not lead anywhere, then you can understand why people feel like that. If it is the beginning of nothingness, then why not ignore that uncomfortable reality and feel happier? If life is only about having as much fun as possible and feeling sad when it ends, then you don't want to think too much about it. You want to go on giggling until you take your last breath.

Death as the start of eternity

But what if death heralds something that is far more important than this life here on earth? What happens if the way you live life here and the choices you make have an effect on the afterlife? What happens if you are finally going to meet God? What happens if there is such a thing as absolute truth and God represents complete purity and righteousness, and what if I know that I don't measure up to those standards? What happens if I've never allowed myself to think through those issues?

If any of the above questions need answering, then surely, we all need time to think about them before we die?

Some of my experiences of ministering to the dying

Fred buried his wife six months ago. She was a devout Christian believer, but he never spent time thinking about religion for himself. As a couple they were very much in love, and suddenly he realised that he might never see her again, and that her faith was important to her.

What to do? It's no good telling a man like that that differences in religion don't matter. He knows perfectly well that they do. It's no good telling him that he has lived just as good a life as his wife. He knows he hasn't. And it's no good telling him to trust to luck and that their love will count for everything. He's not at all sure that it will.

It's only the truth of the gospel which reassures him that, although he might have been wrong in his beliefs and not had any time for God, it's never too late; that the Father is waiting to receive him and put His loving arms around him; that he will be received at the gates of heaven because he's choosing to trust in a Saviour now, and then he will be in heaven for exactly the same reason as his wife – because of the grace of the Lord Jesus who died for him. When he has received that assurance of certainty of an eternal home, he can die in peace.

His relatives were also relieved about the change that came over him in his last days, although they didn't understand his worries.

Patrick had been a man's man all his life. He had an extensive family whom he loved and who had always made a fuss of him. As he was dying, with shortness of breath and heart failure in his own home, he was surrounded by that loving family, but somehow that wasn't enough. He was afraid to tell them of his weakness, but he wanted to know how he could be made right with God.

When I arrived – called by the family, who had contacted the church through the internet, because they couldn't answer any of his questions and they could see that he was in distress – he asked them all to leave the house. He wanted to talk in complete freedom to his new spiritual advisor. 'Don't tell them what we've talked about,' he pleaded. 'I don't want them to know that I'm afraid.'

Afraid of what? Afraid that he hadn't always been honest or done his best? Afraid that he wouldn't be good enough for God? So would the message that he had tried his best and no one could expect any more satisfy him? Of course not! He hadn't always tried his best, because most of the time, like all of us, he wanted things for his own advantage. You couldn't kid Patrick that he had always been 'nice' or 'good'. He knew the truth. He wanted assurance of sins forgiven, and nothing else would do. He was still breathing shakily because of his heart condition when I left the house, but he was breathing as a free man, ready to meet God.

Pete had always been a bit of a lad. He hadn't meant any harm, but he had caused quite a few worries to his family, mainly because of his irresponsible behaviour. When he tried to do better, he always ended up in trouble again. He was always very popular with his mates. Then he was diagnosed with a terminal illness. He was brave on the outside – he'd had his share of the good life – but inside he was ashamed of the way he had let so many people down.

So how does a bad boy face God? Does he laugh it off or shrug his shoulders? Pete had tried doing that, but it didn't work. He knew that he needed to acknowledge his wrongdoing to God and to seek His forgiveness, and even say 'sorry' to others he had hurt.

Can you also get forgiveness for hurting the people who have died without anything being put right? Yes, you can. It's never too late. You can cling to the cross – Pete kept it near him from the moment of his commitment to God. There was no one with him when he died, but the clutch cross was right next to him on the floor, after he returned from the service at the local church.

In the months after his diagnosis, he wanted everyone to know what had happened to him. He told others before he died that he was not afraid now, because he knew that he was going to heaven. 'Make sure my mates know about this,' he told me when he left instructions to conduct his funeral.

'Hold thou thy cross before my closing eyes. Shine through the gloom and point me to the skies,' we sang at his funeral.[52] It was the cross that brought him peace, not a last drink and laugh with his friends, anxious to forget the difficult things in life.

---

[52] Henry Francis Lyte (1793–1847), 'Abide With Me'.

Val had been bedridden for two or three years. She was a very resourceful lady who did not spend her time complaining. In her nursing home, she was easy to look after, and she appreciated the way her family visited her and arranged for her to be entertained by a musician who sang folk songs she knew from her childhood.

One day, the musician invited me to visit her and to listen to the music he was playing for her. It was a great pleasure to meet Val and to hear a bit about her life. Afterwards I offered to pray with her. She assented, and for her it was a new experience to hear someone talking to God as a person, rather than through set prayers.

When, two weeks later, the doctor told her she had about a month to live, she panicked. She had always led a 'good' life, so what would she have to fear? But she did fear. She said that she suddenly realised that she had no idea what she was going to say to God when she met Him. What defence would she have to bring for the mistakes she had made? It was at that point that she remembered the way I had prayed. 'That lady will know what I should say to God,' she thought to herself. The problem was that she did not know my name or where I could be found.

For the first time in her life, she called out to God herself. She said to Him, 'Please find that lady for me,' and she began to question all the care workers. They did not know me, because I didn't often visit that particular home. Then one of them saw me downstairs. She told me about Val's insistent request.

When I went to her bedside, would reassurance from me about her exemplary life have helped her? No. She wanted to know what she should say to God personally. I told her the story of the lost sheep in Luke 15. I told her that we often felt lost, because we had been out of touch with God, but that the Good Shepherd was waiting to receive her and bring her back to the Father. 'When you meet with God,' I told her, 'you don't have to pretend that you were good enough. You only have to say that you are ready to go to heaven, because Jesus has picked you up and carried you. Do you think you could manage that?' She was sure that she could, and so she died in peace.

As we minister to elderly people, we can pray that they will be able to open up to us about their fears, if they want to, even if such fears are dismissed by others. It is an opportunity for us to offer the gift of 'helps' in the slow lane of life.

Fear as bondage

Fear has a weird effect on time. It draws time out, but not in a peaceful way. You can feel as though you are spending hours agonising over whether you are really ill or not, or whether you have done the wrong thing, or whether you have offended someone, or whether you have been cheated. It might just be a matter of minutes in real time, but it feels like hours.

So, if we want to slow down, we don't want to slow time down in this way. We want to have time to be peaceful and joyful. Hebrews 2:14-15 tells us that Satan has spent time binding us to fear, because Satan is the master of death.

I know that I have spent many hours in bondage to the fear of death, and that often produced an intolerable anxiety in my heart. Fear of death can take all sorts of forms. It can take the form of worrying about which illness you might have. At some points in my life, I only had to hear the story of someone with an incurable illness and I was convinced that I too had that illness. I even believed I had started to develop the symptoms. It can take the form of worry that no doctor or person close to you is going to believe you, and so they are going to miss the vital signs of your serious disease. It can take the form of being sure that you are going to be struck by lightning, or being terrified of deep water because you are convinced that in such circumstances you would drown. It can make you terrified to take any risks in case something bad happens to you. It can make you obsessed about safety – convinced that you are going to be knocked down in the road and that you have to take extraordinary precautions to prevent that.

Anxiety works in such a way that you convince yourself that only continued anxiety will prevent anything bad happening to you. If those fears happened all the time, then you would suffer from serious mental illness, but it can happen enough times to deprive you of joy in life. You may even appear to be happy on the outside, but inside you are curled up with fear. Sometimes it is only an escape into films and books or even hard work that enables you to carry on living in a productive way.

This sort of anxiety is linked with the fear of death, and Satan is the master of it. Hebrews talks about the fact that all our lives we have been under the fear of death.[53] I am drawn to the promises in Psalm 94:18-19:

---

[53] Hebrews 2:15.

When I said, 'My foot is slipping,'
your unfailing love, LORD, supported me.
When anxiety was great within me,
your consolation brought me joy.

This reminds me of times in my life when I have been walking through the moorland in winter and my boot suddenly slid on a piece of ice and threatened to destabilise me. It's a picture of how I feel when my troubles seem to be getting too much for me. It is then at such a time when we can experience the Lord's support. Anxiety can be a monster which expands as we give way to it. Knowing the consolation of the Lord at such times brings us peace and joy.

A good death

There is only one person who can release us from the anxiety about death, and that is the person who has defeated death – the Lord Jesus Himself. There is of course the fear of the pain or illness associated with death. Pain in death can often be controlled through good palliative care, and hospices do a wonderful job in allowing people to access this expertise. But we should also be able as Christians to trust God for the way through death.

The famous hymn about grace – 'Amazing Grace' – has this line: 'and grace will lead me home'.[54] Grace is not just about the grace of forgiveness and salvation, but it's also about knowing that Jesus will lead us every step of the way. 'When I tread the verge of Jordan, bid my anxious fears subside', prays another hymn writer, and we need to

---

[54] John Newton (1725–1807), 'Amazing Grace'.

place our trust in God for this.[55] John Donne, the great seventeenth-century Dean of St Paul's Cathedral and poet, has a wonderful poem about his own fear of death, using a play on his last name, 'Donne', to show how God has completed the work of taking him through his fear of death:

> I have a sinne of feare, that when I have spunne
> My last thred, I shall perish on the shore;
> Sweare by thyself, that at my death thy Sonne
> Shall shine as he shines now, and heretofore;
> And, having done that, Thou has done,
> I feare no more.[56]

The early Methodists had a strong belief in a 'good death' and a 'holy death' – one in which someone was able to demonstrate the strength of God and be a witness to others even in death. I've seen this demonstrated in several people I know. I remember being amazed when I was a teenager and visiting a Christian youth leader. She talked about her surgery for breast cancer: 'I thought it was going to be the time when God called me home,' she said, without a shadow of worry. Her certainty and serenity made a big impression on me. I've known people who didn't want to be a burden to anyone when they died, and they had their wish. They died quickly in the night.

[55] William Williams (1717–91), 'Guide Me, O Thou Great Jehovah'.
[56] John Donne (1572–1631) was a poet, sermon writer and Dean of St Paul's Cathedral. From 'A Hymne to God the Father', in John Hayward, ed, *John Donne: Complete Verse and Selected Prose*, Glasgow: The University Press, 1967, pp321-322.

Timing with regard to death

Timing, alongside all our experiences, is in God's hands. '[Our] times are in your hands' (Psalm 31:15) was the frequent saying of my friend's husband when he knew he had terminal cancer. It is not only the possibility of healing or the descent into death which are important aspects of timing, but the way they affect other people around us.

When we were about to move from Manchester to Bristol, one person I was worried about was a dear member of our congregation who had bone cancer and who had been suffering for a number of months. Although it was a terminal prognosis, he drew strength from my visits to him as his church leader. I knew I had to move but I didn't want to desert him in his suffering. I decided that when we moved south, my husband, Mark, and I would travel up to Manchester every month to see him and pray for him and that we would go up if there was an emergency. A month before I was due to move, he passed away in his sleep. Dying for my convenience? I wouldn't be so self-centred as to say so, but it made it much easier for me to settle into my new place of ministry, and before I left Manchester I was able to conduct his funeral and celebrate his life. God has in hand not only the one who is dying but also the needs of those who surround them.

Who will be there when I die?

As three of my children are involved in Christian ministry in other parts of the world, we have talked together about what it will mean if one or both of us, as parents, die without the family there. My own attitude is that the person I really need to be there at my death is the Lord

Jesus. Of course, it's nice to say goodbye to the family, but they are not the ones who take us through to the next world. One of my sons-in-law also pointed out that our moment of death is as a twinkle in the eye compared to the great expanse of eternity when we shall see those we love for ever. My children might miss my death, but we will be reunited in heaven for ever. When the time comes for me to die, the Lord will provide, and it will be far better than any traditional deathbed scene. The Lord Jesus is the one who will take me on from 'the verge of Jordan'.

The wonderful medieval morality play *Everyman* centres round the story of the man (representative of us all) who, finding that he is dying, asks several people to accompany him on his final journey. Friends, family and riches all desert him, either because they don't want to be present or because they are not effective enough companions.[57] In medieval theology it is only 'Church' that can help him through the experience, and what the writer means by 'Church' is the teachings of Jesus at this solemn and dire time of need. I would like to replace the word 'Church' with the name 'Jesus', but essentially this play gets to what is important in death: have we got the right person with us?

One of my parishioners told me two days before she died, when she had to leave her own home and go to hospital in her mid-nineties, that the Lord had come to her in her bed and told her that He was coming for her very soon. She died at peace.

---

[57] Anonymous author, *Everyman*, a medieval morality play, circa 1530. Published in G A Lister (ed), *Three Late Medieval Morality Plays: Mankind, Everyman, Mundus et Infans,* London: Methuen Drama, 2022.

Elijah was caught up to heaven in a chariot (not a bad way to go!), and the person who witnessed it was Elisha. It was only when Elisha saw this great event that he was able to return to his own very powerful ministry, convinced that his mentor had departed at exactly the right time.[58]

We are surrounded by 'a great cloud of witnesses' (Hebrews 12:1) who encourage us as we go through life and into death. They are 'the communion of saints' and, in modern Christianity, some people believe they are encouraging us on our way and understand all that is going on. Using the metaphor of the race, they have passed the baton of witness to us, and we in turn will need to pass it on to others, especially younger people.

How we do that is very important. If we are selfish, we will always be looking to ourselves and stressing our gifts and ministry. If our heart is in the kingdom, we will be looking at training others and encouraging others in the ministry. It doesn't mean we will have nothing to do – there is always enough work for everyone, especially in the area of the gift of 'helps' – but it does mean we should rejoice in the ministry of those who are younger than ourselves, even if we think we could do better than them. There is no room for self-service in the kingdom of God. We shouldn't be irreplaceable in the church until we drop dead, leaving no one adequately prepared for the continuation of ministry.

---

[58] 2 Kings 2:1-17.

Long-term illness

How is our time different when we are facing long-term illness and death is inevitable? Should we be spending our time trying all sorts of cures and wringing our hands, or even going to endless meetings to claim healing? I am not decrying different medications or saying that we cannot ask for supernatural healing from God, but there are lots of other ways of spending our time as we prepare for eternity.

We never stop serving. We can enjoy the Lord's presence at a more leisurely pace. And we can go on praying. Apparently, George Verwer spent the last few months of his life rejecting special medical treatments, instead choosing to pray for others.[59] He always had prayer letters from people around the world which he made use of to engage in intelligent, powerful prayer. What a way to spend the last months of your life!

If we live in a care home, we can spend our time comforting others and making sure their needs are met. I heard the testimony of a young pastor who visited one of his church members in hospital in order to bring comfort and help to her. He left the hospital after she had only wanted to know how his family was progressing and how the church was faring. She assured him that he needed prayer far more than she did, because the Lord had already provided for her and she was going to glory.

My friend has experienced difficulties with her chemotherapy, but she is a veteran prayer warrior, so

[59] George Verwer (1938–2023) was the founder of Operation Mobilisation, www.georgeverwer.com (accessed 17th December 2024).

when recently we have had emergency problems in our family, she is the one I call to get praying. She is lying on her sofa praying for others, and I value her input.

My friend Chris, who lived with pancreatic cancer for two years before she died (it should have been much faster, but the Lord obviously had work for her to do), spent those two years telling people about Jesus and what He had done for her. It was very powerful, not only because she was clearly guided by the Holy Spirit, but also because people automatically listen with respect to someone who is in the process of dying. No one could ignore what she had to say, especially as she said it with grace and a huge amount of down-to-earth humour.

Chris gave me a picture of a walled garden for the time when she was approaching death, and I found it a helpful illustration.[60] Yes, we might know pain and distress, but we can also have lots of pleasure. It's not the pleasure of being able to travel as we wish and stride over the moors in complete freedom. It is a restricted pleasure because there are walls, and we can't escape them. Nevertheless, the garden – with its roses and home-grown vegetables – brings enormous pleasure and we can genuinely enjoy its produce.

If you have ever visited a walled garden outside a great castle or stately home, you will know that it does strange things to your sense of time. Freedom is restricted. You haven't got the opportunity to go galloping across the countryside not caring where you are going. You have to

---

[60] Christians sometimes receive pictures in their minds, which they believe are God-given, and help them to understand spiritual truths better.

deliberately find the flowers or the bushes that bring you pleasure, and you have to stop to smell them or touch them. You are aware of the designer of the garden and what they were hoping to give you – their vision of the world. You enjoy walking the paths or looking at the urns or walking round the maze, but as you look back you are aware of the plan, and you take pleasure in the time you spend there. I think that can happen when you know you are dying. I have a friend in Manchester who knows he has an incurable brain tumour. He has had a major operation and he is now experiencing a very uncomfortable course of radiotherapy, but whenever you see him on Facebook, he is enjoying something, such as a meal out with his wife or a trip to the park with his grandson – and he looks genuinely happy. He is getting the maximum out of every day he has left, as well as looking forward to eternity.

The seed goes into the ground

Jesus said that the seed has to go into the ground and die before it produces fruit and new life.[61] This was first of all true of Himself. He experienced a cruel death, because He knew that it was only through this death that He could rise again and bring about new life for all of us. That night in Gethsemane must have been the longest imaginable as He agonised over what was to come. But He didn't turn back, because He knew that He was going to conquer death.

Like Jesus, we have to go through death. It's the ultimate slowing down process, when 'mind and memory flee',[62] but we slow down so that we can burst forth in

---

[61] John 12:24.
[62] James Montgomery (1771–1854), 'According to Thy Gracious Word'.

exuberant, exciting life again, just as Jesus' resurrection life did. Time has its drawbacks – think of all the occasions when you haven't had time for something you wanted to do – but eternity will have none of these drawbacks. It will give us complete satisfaction and it will never go faster than we want it to. We will be caught up in the eternal moment of love and peace and joy.

If I have to slow down a bit before I can experience that eternity, then it will have been worthwhile. And, while I slow down, I can be involved in ministering to others.

Think about! *Reflections on Bible passages and your own walk with the Lord*

1. Looking at 1 Kings 18 and 19, do you feel as though it is Obadiah's or Elijah's attitude to persecution and death that resonates most with you? Are you someone who relishes the idea of challenge, or someone who would prefer to go down a different pathway?

2. Where would you like to die and who would you like to have around you?

3. Have you had times in your life when you have been overcome by anxiety? How did you cope with that experience?

Think about! *Your own gifts and ministry*

1. Have you had any experience of ministering to the dying? If not, how would you feel about being able to pray with someone before they die?

2. What would you say to someone who tells you that they are afraid of dying? (Not necessarily someone who is old or is expecting to die soon.)

3. Is the timing of death important to family members? Have you seen any examples of that in your pastoral ministry or family experience?

Conclusion

When we look back over our lives, we see lots of threads coming together. It may be that we remember a particular time when God intervened in our lives, or when we chose to turn to Him, but we also see that nothing came into our lives by chance. Truly, as Psalm 139:16 tells us, 'Your eyes saw my unformed body,' and also God knew about the work He was going to give us, as He did with Jeremiah, when he was called to be a prophet before his birth.[63]

In Ephesians 3:15, Paul reminds us that the Father is the one 'from whom every family in heaven and on earth derives its name'. This isn't confined to special, religious families. When we look at the mistakes, or even wilful sins, of our parents or those who influenced us, it may be hard to see that God can bring good out of adverse circumstances, but He can. This should encourage us that nothing happens to us by chance and that God can bring good out of the greatest difficulties.[64]

With this as a foundation for our lives, we can feel free to praise God, enjoy His presence and help others. Anna and Simeon were old people who had been waiting a long time for the Messiah to be revealed, but while they were waiting, they were not wasting their time or feeling sorry

---

[63] Jeremiah 1:5
[64] Romans 8:28.

for themselves. They were in the Temple to worship, to pray and to advise others. If Anna had been doing this from an early age until she was at least eighty-four (her exact age at this point is not made clear in Luke 2:36-38), we know that we can start being used by God when we are young and continue into old age. Being a widow would have been hard in Jewish society, but Anna didn't seem to bemoan her adverse circumstances. Yes, when she saw the Messiah for herself, that would have been a high point, but she had plenty of other moments of fruitful ministry.

May Anna's attitude be true for all of us as we seek to serve God, even in the most inconspicuous of ways. We won't get all our personal problems or intellectual questions sorted out in this life, but we can rejoice in what God gives us to do. And, one day, we will 'know fully, even as [we are] fully known' (1 Corinthians 13:12).